THREE SPANISH HERETICS
AND THE REFORMATION

PAUL J. HAUBEN

THREE
SPANISH HERETICS
AND
THE REFORMATION

Antonio Del Corro — Cassiodoro De Reina —
Cypriano De Valera

GENÈVE
LIBRAIRIE DROZ
11, rue Massot
1967

1re édition: août 1967

CONTENTS

ABBREVIATIONS

AA	Antwerpsch Archievenblad
BCHEW	Bulletin de la Commission de l'Histoire des Eglises wallonnes
BSHPF	Bulletin de la Société de l'Histoire du Protestantisme français
BW	Eduard Böhmer, Bibliotheca Wiffeniana
CR	Corpus Reformatorum
CSP	Calendar of State Papers (*SP:* State Papers)
GN	Christiaan Sepp, Geschiedkundige Nasporigen
HSP	Publications of the Huguenot Society of London
Kerk. St.	C. Sepp, Kerhistorische Studien
NCF	Negociaciones con Francia
PRO	Public Records Office
PSP	Parker Society Publications
Polem.	C. Sepp, Polemische en Irenische Theologie
Pred.	C. Sepp, Uit het Predikantleven van vroegere Tijden
RAE	Luis Usoz y Rio, ed., Reformistas antiguos españoles (also known as Obras de los españoles reformados).
SP	State Papers

Note: In text and notes, except where indicated or very obvious, I have modernized contemporary spelling. In his day Corro frequently was called Corranus, Coran, and the like, all of which were derived from the Latinized del Corro. Similarly Reina often was Reyna, Reinius, etc.

VIII

FOREWORD

This study constitutes a continuation of certain chapters of my doctoral dissertation, " Spanish Protestant Refugees in Western Europe during the Second Part of the Sixteenth Century," done at Princeton University under the guidance of the late E. Harris Harbison. This sensitive man's patience and acuity are known to any who worked with him, and my debt to him is enormous. I am very grateful, too, to his colleague, Professor Joseph R. Strayer, who was familiar with the thesis and has continued to support me warmly in ensuing, related endeavors. Chairman Jerome Blum of this history department also deserves my great thanks in this regard. Although my work with him lay outside this field I doubt very much that I could have gotten through the thesis and post-doctoral studies without having experience the rigorous standards of R. R. Palmer, now Dean of the Faculty at Princeton University.

Professor Edward M. Wilson of Emmanuel College, Cambridge University, directed my attention to the unpublished work of William McFadden, discussed below, without which this study would have been far more difficult than it was to complete. For this and many other things I am in Professor Wilson's considerable debt. Professor John E. Longhurst of the University of Kansas read most of the manuscript and I profited from his intelligent advice throughout; any shortcomings are not his. With regrettable brevity I must record my gratitude also to Professor Haim Beinart of the Hebrew University of Jerusalem, Professor Albert A. Sicroff of Queens College of the City University of New York, Professor Thomas G. Barnes of the University of California,

Berkeley, and most emphatically not least, Professor Hans Rosenberg, now also of the University of California, Berkeley, for bringing the excitement of history to me as an undergraduate. Space forbids mentioning here several others to whom I am anonymously indebted, as it were; I have tried to make amends in the notes.

Successive grants-in-aid from the American Philosophical Society for the years 1964-1966 made this and briefer projects possible, and I am very greateful for this generous assistance. Thanks in this regard are also due the Department of History of Michigan State University for obtaining supplementary funds to forward the study's progress since 1965.

Of my wife Janet, who raised a family and shared the vicissitudes of her husband's years in graduate school and first ones in teaching, while pursuing despite considerable obstacles her own endeavors, this bare recording of her help will have to do. She knows that what I mean cannot be enclosed by words.

PREFACE

There exists no analytical study of the Spanish Reformation heretics since Eduard Böhmer's compilations of nearly a century ago.[1] The reader may well ask why further inquiry into the stories of this handful of relatively insignificant exiles should be useful or necessary, especially considering the Böhmer volumes are far from dated, their age notwithstanding. To some extent this question is answered in the introductory statement opening the long Part I on Antonio del Corro, but here I will try to indicate my feelings on the subject as a whole.

Initially, there is the genuine antiquarianism in such a topic which to the students is its own justification for the study of any segment of the past. In my own case, it must be added, I more of less stumbled into the subject on the doctoral level,[2] to become increasingly fascinated by its numerous attractions. Autobiographical aspects aside, what are these? Corro in particular, and the others to a lesser degree (in large part simply because of the paucity of available materials) are remarkably appealing human beings threading their lives through a most complex age, not entirely unlike our own. In their careers history takes on flesh; we are able to deal with inexorable, often barely visible forces and trends (so necessary for historical analysis and comprehension, however abstract) on the individual and collectively human basis. Such factors alone suggest the subject's compelling interest.

At the start of Part II note that Corro's importance was frequently extrinsic, in that through him and his relations with them we often are in a position to discover new and helpful things about more significant personages. The same holds true for his two peers in this work; that, for most the time, Corro's influential friends and enemies were also those of Reina and Valera's lends added unity to this study. All three began life as Catholic monks, and early on became Calvinists, which suggested the title.[3] Indeed, they all were from the same Hieronymite monastery near Seville, San Isidro del Campo.[4]

Through these three figures to be considered the historical utility of the Spanish Protestant emigrés becomes apparent. Those who escaped Spain and the Inquisition, and others of Spanish lineage concentrated in cities like Antwerp, had sooner or later to scatter across western Europe. With Elizabeth's accession London rapidly became their center, much as it was for most Reformed exiles. Therefore, not only can we obtain fresh views on important individuals linked with these refugees, but, as it were, a grass-roots insight into the Reformation (and Counter-reformation for that matter) at work in many places. Furthermore, their reactions to the presence of such Spanish heretics often revealed governments' policies. The most obvious example would be Elizabeth's[5] shifting attitudes towards them, which usually varied according to the immediate state of Anglo-Spanish relations; equally, official French stances in this regard expressed much of France's ambiguity towards Philip II after 1559.

With the exception (as far as discernible, it should be added at once) of Valera, the Spaniards under study all ran afoul of their new religion sooner or latter. And notably in Corro's case they were liable to find themselves publicity and *simultaneously* charged contradictorily with anti-Trinitarianism (concerning both the Trinity and infant baptism), Anabaptism, " crypto- " Catholicism (or Lutheranism or both), heterodoxy on the Eucharist, and so on. Such remarkable accusations came consistently from the mouths and pens of eminent men like Theodore Beza, Calvin's esteemed successor. Quite as often the Spaniards' defenders were notable laymen, such as William Cecil and the Earl of Leicester in England, and the Colignys in France, as well as respected theologians and prelates like Archbishop Matthew Parker of Canterbury and lesser Calvinist ministers on the continent. Sometimes a man's position in such controversies would alter over a period of years, as did Edmund Grindal's towards Corro, while throughout he favored Reina.

It will not do to assume some lied or were cynical hypocrites, or, in God's name would do anything to bring an enemy of the faith low; although the last perhaps comes very close to the explanation. I have found it most instructive to follow the brilliant reasoning of Lucien Febvre [6] to clarify the mentality behind such situations.

Febvre observed that certain words possessed highly abusive, yet indeterminately emotional meanings in the sixteenth century. "Atheist" was perhaps the most typical.[7] "Servetianism" shortly held similar qualities for Spanish Protestants. Basically, once this sort of charge was levied the accused was guilty almost automatically until proven innocent. Furthermore, it was common to couple one of these extreme pejoratives with a potentially more concrete (if still erroneous) one. Rabelais, for instance, was at one time both an atheist and a Lutheran to Calvin, which led time both an atheist and a Lutheran to Calvin, which led Febvre to comment astutely that " the impassioned religious of the century scarcely hesitated to couple such extraordinary epithets against an adversary whom it was convenient to [permit to leave the faith, voluntarily or otherwise]."[8] Ironically, the Spanish Inquisition, in its successful struggle against Erasmism and Illuminism from approximately 1525-1540 had evolved a similar and brilliantly workable formula, best shown by the case of Juan del Castillo. He had " circulated among the Erasmists at Charles V's Court and the University of Alcala; ... closely associated with the leading apostles of illuminism; ... was burned... as a disciple... of Luther " in 1535.[9] Such " heretical packaging ", accuracy regardless, proved very effective, aided by the split between the Erasmists and Illuminists.[10]

Febvre traced Beza's changing attitudes towards Rabelais,[11] which I believe prefigured his similarly altering views concerning Corro, et al. Initially he was overwhelmed by Rabelais's " talents and philosophy; " subsequently they became " antipathetic and odious " to him when the latter ceased to attack only the Papacy, but began to react also against Protestant excesses and fanaticism. Ultimately, of course, Rabelais placed high on Beza's list of the damned, doubtless the more so since the latter had so misjuged him before. This particularly resembles the development of his relations with Corro.

The great French scholar believe that the vehemence and vituperation marking these confrontations, which allowed little scope for compromise, much less quarter, was part of the Reformation's heritage from the Renaissance. Specifically he referred to the humanists' literary and other quarrels, which displayed this highly personal, abusive form, always far out of proportion to the original difference.[12] Since men like Calvin and Beza had been steeped in humanism, this approach followed, reinforced by the absolute requirements to defend an embattled new faith against enemies (even unwitting ones) from within, not merely from without. Regarding Servetus, most appropriately for us, Febvre observed that the orthodox saw the consequences already in "A", assumed the ensuing potential stages " B-Y", and " condemned 'A' in the name of ' Z ' without the least hesitation."[13] We could well add: without the least insincerity, either. Precisely such sequences will characterize much of the follbwing.

Ordinarily a writer will hardly borrow in bulk from another for his own introduction. But Rudolph Binion's opening remarks for his study struck me as so appropriate to mine that I have excepted handsomely from them to bridge this introduction to the text: " In this book I have attempted to write... history in the form of comparative biography and... of the ' life-thought-and-times ' variety in... continuous narrative. Whether men make history or vice versa, history is not comprehensible unless men are: hence the advantage of approaching the two simultaneously. Likewise, men's throughts and actions are always bound up with each other as well as with their historical context; to view them under separate heads... is ultimately a source of confusion." [14]

---

[1] *BW* (London-Strasbourg, 1874-1904, 3 v; reprinted NY, 1962) relied heavily on the papers of Benjamin Wiffen; this work has stood time's tests extraordinarily well. Böhmer's primary purposes were to provide bibliographical information as to the subjects' works and a mainly descriptive narrative of each man; he rarely placed these people in their broad historical-theological setting. The volumes do, however, give us much useful detail from which to work.

[2] The late Garrett Mattingly suggested the topic to Professor Harbison and myself while he was a Shreve Fellow at Princeton in the fall of 1960. Since I was interest both in Spanish and Reformation history it seemed an ideal way to combine them.

[3] However, it is undeterminable whether Valera ever was a minister. See Pt. II, ch. 2.

[4] On this monastery see Pt. I, ch. 2, notes 1-5. Clearly its proximity to Seville's quasi-heretical conventicle accounted for the Protestantism of Corro and eleven of his fellow monks; no other Hieronymite convent underwent a similar experience, while Judaizing, once the Order's plague, had been eradicated by c. 1500. On the Order and this problem especially see H. Beinart, " The Judaizing Movement in the Order of San Jeronimo in Castile," *Scripta Hierosolymitana* 7 (1961): pp. 167-192; Fr. Jose de Sigüenza, *Historia de la Orden de San Jeronimo* (Madrid, 1907-1909) 2nd ed., 2 v.; A. A. Sicroff, *Les Controverses des Statuts de ' Pureté de Sang ' en Espagne de XVe au XVIIe Siècle* (Paris, 1960): pp. 76 et sqq. especially. Dr. Sicroff is pursuing this subject in several articles. As to why only a dozen of the San Isidrians succumbed to heresy and not all, Michael Walzer's observations in his *Revolution of the Saints* (Harvard University Press, 1965): p. 308 is helpful: "...group experiences [do not] make individual conversion predictable; each of them makes it comprehensible."

[5] I have studied this in some detail in the articles, "A Spanish Calvinist Church in Elizabethan London, 1559-1565," *Church History* 39 (March, 1965): pp. 50-56 and " In Pursuit of Heresy," *Historical Journal* 9 no. 3 (1966): pp. 75-85.

[6] In his *Le Problème de l'Incroyance au XVIe Siècle* (Paris, 1947) 2nd ed. It is shameful that only one of Febvre's many fine works has been translated into English: the Luther book.

[7] *Ibid.*, pp. 139 ff. On p. 149 f he said it was a covering term for general impiety.

[8] *Ibid.*, pp. 134 ff.

[9] John E. Longhurst, " The *alumbrados* of Toledo," *Archiv für Reformationsgeschichte* 45 (1954): p. 234.

[10] E.g. Archbishop Manrique, as Inquisitor-General in 1525, was a noted protector of Spanish Erasmism who led a massive condemnation of Illuminism in which I believe he tried firmly but vainly to dissociate the two in the minds of their common enemies, led by the Dominicans, who staffed and ran the Holy Office. The fact that Manrique was at once a ' liberal ' prelate and head of the Inquisition ought to serve as a reminder that nothing should be stereotyped. That shortly after 1525 the Inquisition began to accuse both successfully of " Lutheranism " suggests, too, that the tribunal's head could not always control its branches if it ..an against commonly-held majo:itarian views in the

rank and file. Manrique's attack on Illuminism merely gained a few years for the Erasmists, given the objective conditions prevailing then in Spain. Although as Castillo's case in n. 9 above indicates, it was possible that while individuals were connected with the two, Erasmism and Illuminism were far from identical. The former relied heavily on the written word, the latter on the inner spirit; both tended to varying degrees to downgrade or minimize the faith's externals without remotely formally repudiating Catholicism. The bibliography on Erasmism is great, on Illuminism very thin. See my article, " Reform and Counter-reform: The Case of the Spanish Heretics," to appear in a forthcoming memorial volume of essays dedicated to Professor Harbison, for some further discussion of these matters.

[11] Febvre, p. 148.

[12] *Ibid.*, pp. 139 ff, 152 f, Interestingly this mentality is portrayed brilliantly in our century in Henri de Montherlant's historical play, *Malatesta*.

[13] R. Binion, *Defeated Leaders* (NY, 1960): p.v.; it studies three French politicians of the early twentieth century. I am indebted to my very able colleague, Dr. Donald N. Baker, for bringing this to my notice.

PART I

ANTONIO DEL CORRO
(1527-1591)

" A Fantastic Spaniard "
and the Reformation

I. INTRODUCTION

Only a few men of the sixteenth century fled the security of a Spanish Hieronymite monastery for the dangers of an itinerant Calvinist life abroad. Of these Antonio del Corro was perhaps most remarkable. He undertook missionary work in France and the Low Countries, after some training at Lausanne, moved to England to be successively a controversial refugee minister in London, theological lecturer at the famous Elizabethan law schools, the Inns of Court, and obtained a similar post at Oxford which occasioned heated debate there. He ended as an Anglican prebend. Not surprisingly wherever Corro appeared he rapidly became " the center of theological controversy," [1] while another modern student has given him the designation we have seen fit to appropriate: " the fantastic Spaniard." [2]

Aside from a real, but minor interest as a rather striking person Corro simply was not of the first rank among Reformation figures. His theology, insofar as it is discernible, was largely derivative, and certainly his written efforts had small impact then or afterwards. If anything his numerous time-consuming battles with various adversaries ranging from Theodore Beza to obscure Calvinists and Puritans clearly prevented him from giving the concentrated attention required for more constructive and possibly profound works, if he possessed that capacity. Therefore, however fascinating his private life and wanderings were—and so much is true—we should justify an extended appraisal of a man like Corro.

Directly put, his importance is, in a sense, largely negative or extrinsic. The fact that Beza took rather great pains to try to

3

undermine him over several years indicates that at least one eminent contemporary did not take him lightly. Corro's range of friends and enemies was enormous, including personages such as the Earl of Leicester, Lord Burghley, Bishops Parker, Grindal, and Sandys, the Châtillon family, Renée of Ferrara, Jeanne d'Albret, and a host of lesser figures stretching from Geneva across France to Antwerp and England. This suggests to us that often through their relations with Corro we can obtain new views of these far more eminent people. Nonetheless, Corro also deserves notice as one of the leading Spanish adherents of the Reformation. While few in number the Spanish Protestants, most of whom were Calvinists, were scattered widely across Europe, and through them we can get something resembling a grass-roots view of the Reformation (and Counterreformation as well) at work.[3] To a considerable extent Corro exemplified this.

The idea that Corro's difficulties as a Protestant stemmed primarily from his supposedly odd theology is usually taken for granted. Such a thesis ties together the vast and sprawling un-published doctoral dissertation by William McFadden which remains the only twentieth century evaluation of Corro in depth.[4] This study relies heavily on McFadden's exhaustive effort, the product of two decades' research, which has greatly supplemented our own, especially on numerous factual details. We do not, however, accept his interpretations at every turn, and in most areas, reinforced by the reading of several of Corro's works, we go our own ways. It is true, however, that led by Beza many charged Corro with one kind of heterodox thought or another, the range of which will be brought out below. But an examination of Corro's writings makes this writer wonder what the real issues at hand were, and increasingly I am driven to the conclusion that to a considerable degree the theological polemics between Corro and his opponents were frequently " ideological " guises for bitter personal dislikes. The problem in part may also be argued in terms of: was there fire when there was so much smoke? The emphasis on personalities over and against doctrinal differences is not as tepid as it may appear, and Corro's own aggressiveness and occasional underhandedness suggest the

4

relevance of this approach. It should also be kept firmly in mind that a Spanish heretic, particularly one of the cloth, was by no means welcomed with open arms into the Protestant camps. Indeed, not only was he constantly made aware of Catholic Spain's continuing interest in his whereabouts, but too often he was considered a follower of Servetus by many Protestants, unless proven otherwise.[5] The popular anti-Spanish feeling in Elizabethan England frequently failed to exempt Spanish heretical refugees from this general opprobrium. To Corro's credit he did not ássimilate and Anglicize as many of his fellows did, nor did he apologize in any way; rather, he fought back. This last trait was a very consistent and sympathetic one, which set him apart from most of the other Spanish Protestants we have studied.

[1] H. C. Porter, *Reformation and Reaction in Tudor Cambridge* (Cambridge University Press, 1958): p. 283.

[2] Eleanor Rosenberg, *Leicester, Patron of Letters* (NY, 1955): p. 135.

[3] See the works of John E. Longhurst and others cited below.

[4] William McFadden, "Life and Works of Antonio del Corro," unpublished PhD. thesis, Queen's University of Belfast (1953). I was able to obtain a microfilm copy which is deposited in the Michigan State University library. While Dr. McFadden generously permitted me to use his materials, he has declined an offer to join me directly in combining our efforts here. Prior to his study the sole survey of Corro, which concentrated on his first London years, was in *BW*, 3: pp. 1-77.

[5] E.g. the author's "A Spanish Calvinist Church in Elizabethan London, 1559-65," *Church History* 34 (March, 1965): pp. 50-56. In the 1740 edition of Gottfried Arnold's *Kirchen und Ketzer Historien*, 1: p. 338 Corro is treated this way. I owe this reference to Dr. Norman Springer of Goshen College.

II. FROM THE MONASTERY
OF SAN ISIDRO TO ANTWERP (1567)

Why did Corro become a Calvinist? Generally most who escaped the bonfires of the autos which began in 1558 chose that Protestant faith even as the Inquisition indiscriminately accused all the Spanish heretics of Lutheranism. It seems to us that the Valladolid and Seville-San Isidro " Lutherans " were actually an ill-defined collection of Evangelical Catholics of a quasi-Erasmist nature and potential Protestants in the very broadest sense of the term. The more actively proselytizing character of mid-century Calvinism and, not least, its greater accessibility to Spain in the south of France and elsewhere account for the initial Calvinism of the Spanish religious refugees.[1]

Corro's background and monastic career are difficult to discern. McFadden followed his subject's sketchy autobiographical remarks which took up the early part of his *Letter to the King* (Philip II).[2] These, however, were written in 1567, at least ten years after Corro's flight from Spain, and the context of that work as a whole calls for a cautionary approach towards them. Pretty clearly his first steps towards heresy must be accounted to his monastery's proximity to Seville, where throughout the 1550's Juan Gil, Constantino Ponce de la Fuente, and others were building the small conventicle destroyed at the decade's end. The monastery also provided other noted heretical emigrés, such as Cypriano de Valera and Cassiodoro de Reina.[3] Obviously a party of the Hieronymites were in constant touch with the Seville group. Corro's *ex post facto* summary suggests he personally became involved on investigating the reasons behind Gil's being sentenced to some months in reclusion during 1552-3; his reading of the man's writings apparently persuaded Corro not only of his innocence but of his superior religiosity.[4] He went on to obtain more dangerous fare through friends, and relations connected with the Inquisition, saying he needed to read one's works in order to refute them. The outcome of such a process, incidentally, makes us comprehend why the Inquisition subsequently strove to seal Spain off as far as possible from outside currents of thought. Corro rapidly mastered the basic ideas of Luther, Melanchthon, and Zwingli's heir, Bullinger. He probably also obtained these materials from intrepid—and clearly heretical—smugglers such as Julián Hernández, a member of the Seville congregation.[5] From all this it appears that Corro, like others at San Isidro and Seville had fused the Evangelical Catholic position of Spaniards like Juan Valdés and Constantino Ponce de la Fuente with the more Protestant one of a Juan Pérez. The former could rail at Papal abuses, the abasement of the doctrine of good works, monastic excesses, while calling for meditation and reading of scriptural writings, often in the vernacular, and stressing God's good-will towards man; the latter added to these points the Protestant reduction of the sacraments, denial of the real presence,[6] and a doctrinal rather than an anti-clerical, ethical assault on the Papacy, monasticism, and so forth. If Corro's belated recollections were accurate, and we cannot altogether deny them considering the paucity of other evidence, then San Isidro truly was a " focal point of Erasmism *and* Reform." [7]

Some dozen monks from San Isidro slipped out of Spain during the late summer and early fall of 1557,[8] While there are some grounds for assuming they had foreknowledge of the coming inquisitorial assaults [9] it is odd, apparently, that none were in any position to warn the nearby Sevillans. On the other hand it was entirely possible that the bulk of the latter did not consider themselves Protestants or heretics at all and subsequently were dumbfounded at their arrests on such charges which began with the capture of the aforementioned Julián Hernández on October 7, 1557 and continued through the winter and spring. Meanwhile Corro and his companions, traveling by different routes, attained their pre-determined objective by year's end: Geneva.[10] When we consider that these men of the cowl, lacking prior knowledge of the " world " made their ways across completely unknown and often dangerous stretches of land and sea their collective feat achieves heroic proportions, and reminds us of the spectacular vicissitudes of Reformation refugees in general. The international watchfulness of the Inquisition, the Argus of the period, added a special and ever-present hazard.[11] The escapees' choice of Geneva as their destination forces us back to the matter of why Corro and others of similar history opted for a Calvinism of which they knew little or nothing, as far as is known. Certainly Geneva was not especially safe militarily as the recurring Savoyard threat showed. So it was not mere safety which brought the Spaniards, and of course others, there. The fact that Corro entered the famous Calvinist training ground, the Academy of Lausanne in February, 1558, suggests the likelihood of a deliberate religious choice beforehand. What lay behind that unfortunately remains unknown but for speculation. Clearly the solution to this, if and when forthcoming, will reflect back a good deal of light on the situation at San Isidro and among the Seville and Valladolid groups prior to their breakup and destruction, the contemporary charge of " Lutheranism " notwithstanding.

Corro studied at the Academy of Lausanne, then graced by teachers such as Theodore Beza, from early 1558 until July, 1559.[12] Intensive study in theology, Greek, Hebrew, and the Arts (which included rhetoric, arithmetic, and astronomy based on authors such as Cicero, Aristotle, and Euclid) characterized the curriculum. Bi-monthly theological disputations by the students under professorial guidance presumably enlivened the grind of book-work, and given Corro's subsequent talent in this direction his Lausanne days must have been very useful. In effect he was a ward of the state of Berne, and lived on a ten-florin monthly allowance. Curiously the cantonal authorities at this time required only a civic oath of loyalty to Berne, and not a subscription to its Confession of Faith.[13] However, Corro's matriculation coincided with a prolonged controversy between the Zwinglian Bernese Senate and Viret-led Lausanne academicians over the latter's more rigorous view of election, and more directly, their attempt to implant a Genevan style of examining parishioners before admitting them to communion. The running squabble proved fatal to the Academy, most of whose leading instructors, Beza included, resigned rather than conform to the Senate's orders in the matter. It was reconstituted at Geneva.[14] Later Corro was to deplore what he considered hair-splitting, destructive theological controversy. That does not mean he sided with the " Erastians " at Lausanne.[15] Nothing during this time indicates Corro was anything but an orthodox Calvinist. In fact on April 19, 1559 he applied to Calvin himself for a recommendation to the Albret court at Nérac and Pau in Navarre-Béarn, and on May 26 this was granted.[16] It seems likely he would have checked with people in Geneva who had known Corro, as well as his Lausanne teachers, Beza among them. One cannot believe John Calvin gave endorsements lightly.

Corro arrived at the Albret court sometime in the fall of 1559, where his first assignment was to teach Spanish to the young prince, the future Henri IV.[17] What his other duties were are not clear, although it is hard to believe that a Lausanne alumnus did no more than linguistic tutoring to a six-year old in a region marked by a great spurt in revolutionary Calvinism. Beza himself arrived in August, 1560 to hasten its spread.[18] There is a faint possibility Corro preached in Spanish at Nérac, although not a whit of evidence exists pointing to the presence of any Spanish heretics besides himself.[19] Whatever the case Corro did obtain the lasting good will of Queen Jeanne, who subsequently demonstrated sympathy for him and other Spaniards, such as Reina.[20] Despite this, her husband's growing religious and personal lukewarmness caused a temporary halt to Calvinization, and when Anthony and Louis of Condé were summoned to Orleans on treason charges in the fall of 1560 the faith's leaders scattered and went underground. The brevity of this respite was shown when Jeanne publicly took Calvinist communion later that year, but Corro had by then already assumed his new post as Principal of the College of Aire.

Inspired by Jeanne d'Albret's promotion of Calvinism not far off to the south adherents of the new faith at Aire-sur-l'Adour and adjacent regions literally seized control there during 1561, and it is plausible to think Corro's appointment was due to her favor.[21] Very shortly, however, he was in touch with the Hispano-Portuguese colony at Bordeaux, and probably by October had settled in the southwestern metropolis. It seems pretty clear that his purpose in moving to the inflamed southwest of France had little to do with tutoring Prince Henry or heading a minor educational institution. In fact Corro had hoped originally to found a Spanish Calvinist Church in the presumed security of a Huguenot area, and there is some indication that Calvin himself had looked to the Albret lands as a potential home for fleeing Spanish heretics.[22] Jeanne d'Albret's delicate relations with Philip II nullified such a prospect regardless of her personal feelings which must have been favorable.[23] Corro broadly expressed similar hopes for the southwest as a whole in his pre-viously cited letter to Calvin of October 27, 1561. He even talked of having invited Spanish exiles to the Bigorre to form a church under him, but had had no response. One assumes he referred to the marranos of Bordeaux, shortly to be dealt with, but he is very vague here.[24] Corro asked Calvin for a further testimonial to the Calvinist ministers of Bordeaux so that at their next colloquy he could plead his case for a new church with the master's powerful support.[25] In this letter he used for the first time the pseudonym Bellerive,[26] a common practice among ministers as they traveled about in dangerous territories. Corro's passionate concern with his fellow nationals is very much to the fore in this letter to Calvin, sounding a note which will grow with time.

Among the leading families in the Hispano-Portuguese New Christian group at Bordeaux were the Lopez de Villeneuve and the Bernuy. We have closely studied the Antwerp branches of these families elsewhere in connection with the origins of the Dutch Revolt and the propagation of Calvinism in the Low Countries and Spain.[27] Other members of these clans played similarly prominent roles at Toulouse. In conjunction with the Pérez of Antwerp these marrano families, connected by marriage generation after generation, but prolific enough also to marry into the surrounding urban and rural upper classes,[28] used their international entrepreneurial firms to further Calvinism's spread. Nominally most were Catholics, although in 1550 Henry II had issued a statute recognizing that they constituted a separate " nation " with its own, respected customs.[29]   In conjunction with other developments of the day this pronouncement seems to have served as a quasi-legitimate opening for the Bordeaux marranos to have a fairly free hand in many areas, religion included, on the eve of the religious wars. No doubt their successful commercial and financial dealings enriched the royal treasury and contributed to the region's prosperity greatly; such factors apparently account for Henry's out of character tolerance for a group notorious even outside the Iberian peninsula for its occasional clandestine relapses into Judaism.

Corro's arrival in Bordeaux coincided with relatively halcyon days for Calvinism there; by January, 1562 the faith could be practiced freely just outside its walls. However, Corro's presence caused reactions other than what he, at least, had expected. La Fromentée, the leading Calvinist minister, wrote Calvin in the winter of 1561-62 about the Spaniard.[30] In the course of requesting additional information about him La Fromentée noted that Corro's " life and work are suspect to us... He wants, in fact... to erect another Spanish Church." We must assume that by " another Spanish Church " La Fromentée meant the probably clandestine meetings of the marranos, unless evidence eventually is disclosed to prove something else. Perhaps in Corro's previously-cited letter of the fall of 1561 to Calvin his appeal to " Spanish exiles " had a concrete meaning no longer traceable. These two letters strongly suggest the need, and utility, of further research in this field. Nothing in La Fromentée's letter pinpoints just why Corro was " suspect," and the general feeling one gets from reading it is that the Bordeaux Calvinist clergy resented the possibility of a new, Spanish congregation which apparently might be autonomous in relation to themselves. A definite nativism informs the note. This coupling of vaguely-worded accusations of heterodoxy with more forthrightly-put fears of the " foreigner " who would possibly cause a drop in the membership of one's own church (es) or "erect" a semi-independent one in one's region was from the onset, as this incident showed, to characterize the complaints about Corro. The combination of this hostility from within, which did not, however, come from the marranos, and a violent Catholic reaction in the city ended Corro's still-born mission. The majority of his would-be supporters confined their activities to book smuggling and the like, as quietly as possible.

Corro's next stop was Toulouse, where he took the oath as a Calvinist minister on March 16, 1562.[31] As in the Béarn, at the College of Aire, and at Bordeaux he entered a territory seething with religious tumult owing largely to recent Calvinist forwardness, legal or otherwise. Odet de Nort, the leading Calvinist minister in the city, and a recent arrival himself had written at once to Calvin appealing for additional clergy to spread and strengthen the faith in the Toulousain, given its sudden, striking successes early in 1562.[32] While Corro's local sponsor was one Barthélemy Prévost, *procureur* of the Parlement and a deacon of De Nort's congregation, the possibility that he was of those recommended from Geneva in response to De Nort's February plea for ministerial help cannot be ruled out. This in turn suggests that at Bordeaux Corro's "personal" rather than supposedly "doctrinal" faults had been the core of the matter there. There is no indication, incidentally, that Calvin replied to La Fromentée's letter. The added fact that De Nort, an impeccably orthodox Calvinist, remained Corro's good friend until at least 1564 is another interesting detail in evaluating the Spaniard at this time.[33] On the other hand the Toulouse situation did not remotely allow Corro an opportunity to build a Spanish church as such; therefore, he represented no threat to any established congregation as, apparently, he had at Bordeaux. Nonetheless, somewhat later he was to be accused retroactively of assuming the ministry at Toulouse improperly, which remained an unproven, and discarded charge in the upshot.[34] The flimsiness of this kind of attack was to be typical.

While in Toulouse Corro naturally became intimate with the same kinds of persons he had had support from in Bordeaux. In

12

particular he associated with relatives and friends of the marranos of the latter city who played similar roles at Toulouse, persons such as Jacques de Bernuy and Madame Saint Estienne.[35] Paralleling their situation in the southwestern center the Toulousain marranos had attained prominence: in 1559 Jacques de Bernuy, following in his father's path politically as well as commercially was named President of the Parlement's Court of Inquiry.[36] Persons so placed and favorably disposed towards the new religion could and did assist its growth. But as at Bordeaux a severe Catholic reaction curtailed this process, and the religious discretion exercised by men like Bernuy failed to shield them fully from strong suspicions on the part of the triumphant Catholics.[37] Monluc's entry into the city on May 18 was followed by widespread proscriptions of leading Calvinists, Corro among them; but the experienced Spaniard had already flown the coop - again.[38]

No direct evidence exists to determine Corro's whereabouts from May, 1562 through the following winter. Possibly he went directly to the Béarn, where he had been so hospitably received earlier, although it is not certain he had reentered the Albret lands until early in 1563. During his wanderings that region's Calvinization had proceeded vigorously under Queen Jeanne's auspices, freed by her husband's death from whatever religious restraint that bond may have entailed. Early in 1563 a delegation of Geneva-trained Basque and Béarnese clergy arrived in the region to further the faith. They were led by Jean-Raymond Merlin, one of Corro's former instructors at Lausanne.

It is through him, so to speak, that Corro reentered the records. In his July 23, 1563 letter to Calvin discussing the general situation in the area, Merlin touched on Corro.[39] From this it seems the latter had been preaching under Merlin's jurisdiction for an undetermined period of months, probably from shortly after the Genevan group's above-noted arrival. Corro apparently had heard he was being maligned in Geneva, and had reported as much to Merlin. The small number of Spaniards at Geneva were aroused on behalf of their compatriot, and it is interesting that the accuser has been called by one of the leading scholars of Spanish Protestantism " an ignorant man " who concluded,

13

however, that despite him Corro's "innocence had been recognized."[40] Böhmer seems to interpret this grave charge of Servetianism as coming from within Geneva, however. But the only known definite hostility shown Corro in writing up to this time was from La Fromentée at Bordeaux, whose letter Calvin did not answer as far as is known; with McFadden we believe this episode was a belated echo of La Fromentée's note which may have come to the attention of someone other than Calvin and which could easily have been taken at face value.[41]

Merlin's colleagues, apprised of the matter, requested him to draw up a paper about Corro and forward it to Calvin, which was done by way of the July 23 letter. Given Corro's temperament and his reaction later to somewhat similar occasions, as well as Merlin's remarks, it is highly plausible to think Corro himself asked for a judgment on the accusation from Geneva, which presumably would have silenced all enemies within Calvinism. From Merlin's summary we learn that local pastors appointed to study Corro's beliefs and deeds rapidly dismissed the deadly charge of Servetianism, commenting in passing on the theological incompetence of the accuser. The probable original plaintiff, La Fromentée, had since been martyred, and no one is named. But the Bearnese ministers' analysis of such a charge against Corro is interesting, especially in view of the several similar situations to be described later. In general they found nothing doctrinally amiss with Corro, nor with his morals (he had married during his first stay in this region). Merlin remained neutral about the vague accusation concerning Corro's supposedly incorrect election to the clergy at Toulouse, which seems to reflect a division of opinion among the investigators on this point.[42] Despite all this Corro had already left the area, having been releved at his own request. He had demonstrated a curious restlessness, to the extent of refusing to stay at assigned clerical positions in various villages.[43] The itinerant nature of this recent past seems a flimsy reason behind his indiscipline, yet it is the only one at hand. For this reason, and to all appearances for it alone, the Béarnese pastors were not overly unhappy at losing his services. In Reformation Calvinism there was little or no room for a man, however able, who would or could not follow orders. Puzzlement, more than anything else, characterized the statements passed on by Merlin to Calvin in the assessment of all this, but nothing available indicates that the latter ever entertained doubts about this odd Spaniard. The letter ended by observing that Corro had left the Béarn in the entourage of one Monsieur de Boesse, from the Périgord. A final reflection on the Merlin letter is relevant. Some years later, on the eve of Corro's break with Calvinism, Beza was to write him that he didn't " recall having heard " about the " controversy " between Corro and Merlin![44] It is inconceivable Beza would not have been aware of the situation in the summer of 1563 revolving around Corro, the Béarn, Bordeaux, and Geneva. To misread it as a strong difference between Merlin and Corro was incredible. The certification of his orthodoxy in the Béarn was to be the last he ever received from French Calvinism; Beza's interpretation of it would be one more blow hastening Corro's departure from a faith he had intensely been committed to.

The estates of M. Escodéca, Sieur de Boesse, were near Bergerac, the Huguenot center of the Périgord. How Corro first entered into relations with him is unknown. The importance of his stay in this region lies in his Théobon letter of December 24, 1563 to his old San Isidrian compatriot, Cassiodoro de Reina, then in London, which was one of many written to him.[45] Part of it discussed the projected translation of the Bible into Castilian. From Corro's allusions to previous notes the question of who should join whom remained undecided by this date. Corro indicated he needed a decision on this also to mollify his patrons and his congregation who apparently were not pleased with his casual attitude towards his ministerial duties. One thinks here of the single sustained complaint against him in the Béarn. Corro said that should he be able to present a solid reason to them for his seeming dalliance, such as their proposed joint biblical endeavor, he felt he could also enlist local support in its printing. He added in this connection his optimism about help from Jeanne d'Albert—his tutoring of Prince Henry bore perhaps unexpected rewards.[46] An index of Corro's substantial connections despite his difficulties at Bordeaux and in the Béarn was the itinerary he suggested to Reina should the latter leave England to join him. Reina should sail from Flanders to Bordeaux or La Rochelle unless he prefers an overland journey across France, or down the Rhine valley. Corro named merchants in Antwerp and Bordeaux on whom he could rely, undoubtedly Corro's marrano acquaintances, as well as his old friend from Toulouse days, De Nort, now ministering in La Rochelle.[47] The enthusiasm marking Corro's remarks on the business of biblical translation reminds us anew of what the vernacularization of Scripture meant during this period, and of the translator's dedication and profound sense of mission. To men like Corro a Castilian Bible would be something like the first blast of the trumpet before Jericho; the necessity to observe pastoral cares in the Périgord receded very much to the background in light of such an undertaking, however potential.

None of the above as such subsequently affected Corro's life in England. Rather, another section discussed shortly proved a bed of thorns for Corro and others. How and why this came about has its own interest. Corro was accustomed to having one of his Bordeaux friends, the merchant Pierre du Perray handle his correspondence. The latter sent letters destined for England to a Jacques Fichet for delivery to Reina. Fichet was a refugee Huguenot merchant who belonged to the French Calvinist Strangers' Church of Threadneedle Street in London. The Théobon note reached him about two months after Reina had fled England rather than face a remarkable collection of accusations ranging from Servetianism to adultery and sodomy.[48] On March 12, 1564 the dutiful Fichet deposited the letter with the French Consistory, and subsequently Jean Cousin, pastor of the church, contented himself with a note to Corro explaining that Reina had left the country. He omitted to say why.[49] In fact the suspicions of Cousin and his associates had been aroused merely because Corro wrote Reina. Examination of the " theological " section of the Théobon letter increased their doubts about its sender on internal grounds. As of the spring of 1564 absolutely nothing pointed towards Corro's eventual settlement in London; exactly three springs later he did. This document was there, and the French used it as a springboard to harass him nearly to the end of his days. To Corro, and perhaps to a modern reader Cousin's action, and more so his brief note of " explanation " to Corro smack of very bad faith. But it is inconceivable he acted without consulting his peers and gaining their approval. From the Consistory's view a friend of Reina's was virtually guilty until proven innocent, and I believe it was particularly easy for these men, considering the times, to find some of Corro's remarks theologically offensive given their general context in a letter addressed to a man like Reina. Most men of the major faiths of the period would have acted similarly. In their embattled position they found the hint of heterodoxy unbearable, and this could and did include dangerous associations. One breach of orthodoxy might open the gates to a flood of disasters; toleration certainly was out of the question. But from Corro's position the impounding of his correspondence was unwarranted, especially given Cousin's disguising of the real situation in London concerning Reina. The latter, on the other hand, was an old and trusted friend and a potential collaborator on a project of momentous significance for the evangelization of Spain. That such a private letter should later turn up as the trump weapon against himself was to be unforgivable. To some extent the issue was a clash of two rights: the public and general one of the Calvinist clergy's need to defend the faith and Corro's individual one of privacy and the right to fair dealing. Most men of the Reformation, however, supported the former's primacy. This issue became an implicit part of the Corro affair, and the reader should bear it in mind to comprehend the often unusual bitterness marking his English career.

The passages in the Théobon letter which aggrieved the London French can easily be summarized. Corro had sent Reina some money to buy works apparently unobtainable in the Périgord. Specifically, he requested books by Kaspar Schwenkfeld and his disciple, Valentin Krautwald, and in passing indicated his familiarity with the ideas of Andreas Osiander. All three were notorious heresiarchs, originating within Lutheranism, and Calvinism regarded them with equal distaste. The name of Servetus appeared nowhere in the letter, but from certain hypothetical questions Corro had addressed to Reina in it Beza deduced afterwards the presence of a vague Servetian tendency.[50] Corro also laid himself wide open to criticism when he asked Reina to tell him about Justus Velsius and Giacomo Concio (Acontius), two highly controversial contemporary thorns in the sides of the refugee churches of London. The last notable mentioned in this letter was the Lutheran divine, Johan Brenz, important in the formation of the ubiquitarian theology, to which Calvinism was very hostile. From all this one is reminded of Corro's native inquisitiveness about theological matters first demonstrated in his youthful reaction to the Juan Gil case. In the 1550's he had seen nothing amiss in using his connections to obtain forbidden religious literature on whatever pretext was available. To all appearances he considered himself a loyal Calvinist at the time he wrote the Théobon note (and for some years afterward, as we shall see), and to him the request for such a recondite array of works represented nothing more than the continuation of his wide-ranging exploration of all available religious sources. The Academy of Lausanne apparently had failed to impress upon him the notion that a good Calvinist ought to confine his readings to the works of Calvin and the other leaders of the faith, any more than he had been able to conform to the normal clerical discipline demanded of him in the Béarn and elsewhere, as we have seen. To Jean Cousin and Theodore Beza Corro's queries in this letter smacked all too clearly of a mind toying dangerously with problems about Christ's nature, his mission, and the like, problems which had no business arising in the thoughts and deeds of a true Calvinist. In Corro's formal writings from 1567 he will indeed strike notes which were un-Calvinist, often mixed in with apparently orthodox statements on many other points. We think had he not been subjected to the treatment he received on arriving in London because of his association with the discredited Reina it is quite possible his drift from Calvinism would not have begun in the first place. But as we have stressed, merely to write Reina in 1563 was enough to commence that process.

One other point requires comment. It is best summarized by the following observation: "The wide extension of travel during the latter half of the sixteenth century was... a factor contributing to the development of legal toleration. Travelers were impressed with the absurdity of the existence of a half dozen exclusive 'truths' in Europe, all supported by varying degrees of repression... [and] above all [such men] acquired a comprehensive view of religion." [51] We must hasten to note that most "travelers" were involuntary ones, as Corro frequently was, and the average religious refugee hardly cared about any remote sort of toleration in this sense. Nonetheless, the statement holds true for some, and very likely Corro among them. The gathering irenic tone characterizing his writings obviously derived from both his considerable wanderings before 1567 and his long, hard experience of the "varying degrees of repression."

Sometime during the spring of 1564 Corro received Reina's request for aid in Orleans.[52] He obtained six weeks' leave from the Périgord and joined his compatriot for a private conference with the eminent Calvinist minister, Nicholas des Gallars, Sieur de Saules. Gallars had been Cousin's predecessor and had attended the Colloquy of Poissy in 1561 with Reina. Despite the paucity of evidence on this brief encounter it does appear that Corro assisted Reina in trying to clear the latter of the doctrinal charges made against him in London the previous winter, but without success.[53] As we have shown elsewhere Reina never lived down having fled England without confronting his accusers.[54] It also is reasonable to assume Gallars added to the London French leaders' suspicions of Corro arising from the Théobon letter by informing them of his role on Reina's behalf at Orleans. Obviously, too, Reina had to tell Corro at least a part of his tribulations in London, but the latter apparently failed to forsee just how he would be connected with his fellow countryman by the same people. From Orleans Reina accompanied Corro back to Bergerac, where the latter and a native pastor admitted him to communion.[55] Both Spaniards found it necessary to leave the area sometime after November 26, 1564, which date marked the beginning of the enforcement of the recent edict forbidding both Catholics and Calvinists to use foreign ministers.[56] Shortly before, however, the local Huguenots had invited Renée, Duchess of Ferrara and one of the ranking adherents of the new religion in France to come to the Périgord to support efforts to sidestep this edict.[57] She came down from her castellany at Montargis for a brief visit at Bergerac, and wrote letters on behalf of the inhabitants to Burie, the royal governor, and the King. Almost certainly she met Corro during this journey, and obviously was impressed with him. With Reina in his company Montargis was his next port of call, where he stayed some one and a half years. Reina merely passed through and soon continued on to havens further east.[58]

Renée's unusually non-dogmatic yet irreproachably Calvinist views must have made Montargis very congenial for men like Corro, and his fellow Spaniard, the highly regarded Juan Pérez who was also taken on by the Duchess at this time as her private chaplain.[59] Montargis almost certainly was the hothouse of Corro's later publicly expressed irenicism, and in his mistress he had a living example that such an attitude did not have to deviate from orthodoxy. What he failed to take into account was that her high station as a *princesse royale* not only protected her from Catholic wrath, but undoubtedly caused the Calvinist leadership to treat her tolerant practices and other matters very leniently. Besides, Calvin himself had been instrumental in bringing her to the faith, and always directly concerned himself with her and her affairs.

François de Morel, Sieur de Collonges, had as early as 1554 been sent by Calvin to Renée, and he joined her at Montargis in the spring of 1561 where he was when Corro and Pérez supplanted him. Morel apparently had increasingly fallen out with the Duchess who found the two Spaniards much more to her taste. Among other things she viewed the Frenchman's intemperate attacks on the Papacy and Catholicism generally with alarm since her castellany was in a largely Catholic region and she hardly desired to draw Catholic attention and interference her way on any pretext. Morel also was criticizing her leniency towards Catholic sufferers from the religious wars while she forestalled his efforts to install a Genevan style discipline. It seems likely that Renée preferred, like most aristocrats, to control her church as far as possible, and that her toleration of Catholics derived both from an irenic humanitarianism and her politique approach to keep Montargis the privileged Calvinist sanctuary in a Catholic area it was. Matters came to such a pass that Calvin promised a replacement for Morel, but his death just afterwards and Renée's travels in the south already mentioned prevented this. Shortly after the Spaniards' arrival Renée dismissed Morel herself while the appointment of Corro and Pérez was ratified by the ministers of Montargis and Châtillon, and by the famous three Coligny brothers of the region. Among the members of the Synod of Vertueil which condemned Corro in 1567 was Morel, who claimed to have heard him preach a heretical sermon at Montargis; Corro suggested rather that spite was the man's motive for this later action, and this certainly makes sense in view of the foregoing.[60] Throughout his life Corro was to find a former or present accuser among his judges, and he reacted accordingly. Meanwhile he preached to Renée and her little court, and had the rare opportunity to observe his mistress's numerous works of charity and good deeds at close range. These included the sheltering of refugees, medical supervision during the fighting, secular and religious instruction to the local children, and financial help to the needy and uprooted, all the while maintaining peace within largely Catholic Montargis itself. Yet she was a Calvinist. The approximately twenty months he in her service must have put the finishing touches to Corro's rather individual, yet not necessarily heterodox brand of Calvinism —a faith already threatened unknowingly by the Théobon letter resting in the London French Church. The Montargis idyll closed with Corro's voluntary departure for Antwerp, where the lure of evangelizing Spaniards resident proved overwhelming. To understand how this came about we must backtrack a little.

On may 28, 1566 Renée received a letter from the Antwerp Calvinists requesting Juan Pérez's services.[61] To ask for a Spanish-born Calvinist to come to the most religiously explosive of Philip II's domains suggests the Antwerpers' misreading of the situation. Indeed the letter's text revealed that somehow they thought the presence of such a minister would be more palatable to the regime than the customary use of Huguenot pastors on mission. One would have supposed the Netherlanders by now had a surer insight into Spanish thinking on such a subject; in the very near future they obtained a more accurate view. The writers lauded Pérez's well known scholarship, probity, and past successes in handling difficult situations.[62] Initially the Duchess must have been reluctant to part with her Spanish preachers, for at least as early as August 13 Corro was invited to come with Pérez in the course of a renewed application.[63] The Antwerpers may have learned by then of the aged Pérez's increasing illness. They also probably knew of the technical loophole in the impending September Accord, which was to bar from their city all clergy not subjects of Philip II, and which allowed thereby others with Pérez's status to be called upon. On September 18 Charles de Nielle, a leading Antwerp pastor, implored Corro to labor for the faith in his city.[64] Among other things, he noted the possibilities for the proselytization of Spanish and Italian residents in Flanders and Brabant. Finally the matter was brought before the Colignys and the ministers of Montargis and Châtillon who had confirmed the Corro-Pérez appointments in the first place; all agreed Antwerp had greater need of their services.[65] In passing we note that in a small way this episode further demonstrated Admiral Coligny's realization that the fate of the Huguenots was intimately bound to that of their brethren to the north, and adumbrated his policy on the eve of St. Bartholomew's. On October 12 Corro left, with Renée's instructions to check on Pérez who had gone ahead to Paris to oversee some forthcoming publications then in press. On October 20 Corro wrote her about Pérez's death just after his own arrival.[66] Before continuing on to Antwerp Corro became briefly involved with the complex unscrambling of Pérez's goods, most of which were left to the Duchess, except for a fund set aside for the financing a future complete Castilian Bible, a project Pérez had never finished himself. The oral, and so intestate nature of his will caused some hard feelings between Corro and the two Spanish assistants who had been working with Pérez in Paris,[67] but this seems to have blown over soon and Corro arrived in Antwerp around November 1.

Almost immediately he was confronted with a problem of conscience. Assigned to the Walloon Church, then particularly shorthanded, he was presented for signature by his colleague, Jean Taffin, the Netherlandish Confession of Faith by Guy de Brès, which closely resembled the standard French version. At first Corro readily agreed, but noticed a clause requiring him to condemn the " left wing " of the Reformation. He refused, and unwittingly gave his subsequent enemies in London another weapon.[68] His inability to accept formally the usual denunciations of groups like the Anabaptists and Schwenkfeldians placed him radically apart from the ordinary Calvinist clergy of the time and place. But the Antwerpers seemed not to be bothered by this negative act, and it hardly seems plausible to explain their passivity in this regard solely in terms of their stringent need for qualified ministers. On the other hand the Théobon note had not yet been publicized in the Calvinist milieu. Except for the virtually discredited inquiry into his activities apparently engineered by the late La Fromentée, nothing in Corro's past —or present up to this moment—gave most orthodox Calvinists cause for alarm. His relations with personages such as Jeanne d'Albret, Renée of Ferrara, and Calvin himself were seemingly sure indices of his reliability and doctrinal correctness. His talents as a preacher were widely esteemed. Corro's one previous experience of oath-taking at Lausanne, as well as his recent lengthy sojourn at Montargis, could not have prepared him for the draconian statement he found so offensive in De Brès's document. In this, as in most matters, a currently innocuous action became a heterodox gesture in the eyes of future opponents in other circumstances.

Aside from a few eminent persons like Marcus Pérez and Martin Lopez, Corro found few Spanish Calvinists to work with in Antwerp.[69] It is likely he preached to this select elite of Calvinized marranos privately and in Spanish. But the Antwerpers' expectation of using him publicly ran aground, but for one

23

occasion.   Shortly after Corro's arrival the Walloon Church requested Count Hoogstraten, Orange's deputy at the head of the municipal government, to administer the civic oath to the Spaniard to legalize his status.[70] Hoogstraten and the magistracy hedged, claiming among other things that his long stay in France had disqualified him, and that Spaniards and Netherlanders were actually foreigners in one another's territory, their common overlordship notwithstanding.   Technically this curious bit of political theorizing violated the September Accord, as the heads of the Walloon Church pointed out in their heated reply.   They suggested that to deny Corro proper status would undermine the Accord and open the door to numerous other violations by the concerned parties.   Their note also apologized should its tone " annoy " the king; clearly they knew not their sovereign any more than the knew them.   Disconcerted, Hoogstraten said he would refer the matter to Orange, the city's Burgrave.   As the documents show, the hapless Count was also under great pressure from Brussels to stop what appeared from there the local compromising over Corro.[71]   Meanwhile Corro preached publicly on December 1, mainly because of Taffin's indisposition.[72] This aroused the wrath of the resident Spanish Catholic merchants and bureaucrats, and apparently led directly to the rapid conclusion of Corro's public usefulness to his faith.[73] But Hoogstraten and those on the scene knew the folly of an arrest, which would have engendered an anti-regime riot, and ignored the Regent's repeated admonitions to banish or confine Corro.[74] Meanwhile Orange continued to sit on the entire affair while Hoogstraten wrestled with the Walloon Church's second request at the end of December to administer the civic oath to the Spaniard.   He suggested to the Regent that failure to do so would destory the September Accord and the uneasy peace that document had obtained;[75] he himself clearly refused to take any responsibility beyond delaying tactics.   The Regent demurred, repeating arguments already mentioned in somewhat greater detail.[76]   The Antwerpers then bypassed both Hoogstraten and Brussels with a direct appeal to Orange in Amsterdam; the latter returned to Antwerp on February 5, 1567.   As far as one can tell he took no action to resolve Corro's position. Of course he was a Lutheran at this time, and as always, more concerned with achieving a non-denominational resistance to the regime. In a half-way manner Corro was working along the same line.

We have dealt elsewhere with Marcus Pérez's sponsorship of meetings between Lutherans and Calvinists in fruitless attemps to bring about a united Protestant front in Antwerp.[77] Corro's role in them was prominent, and his maiden written effort reflects his participation, and disappointment in their outcome. It also underlined his close relationship with the Calvinist marranos like Pérez and Lopez, whose relatives in the south of France had sustained Corro earlier. The *Letter to the Lutheran Ministers of the Flemish Church of Antwerp* further testified to the great impact his year and a half at Montargis had had upon Corro. It first appeared on January 2, 1567 in French at Antwerp, and other editions in Dutch and English followed through 1577.[78] A fumblingly quasi-politique approach informed this pamphlet, and as such it satisfied very few. A typical excerpt proclaimed " it was a most deplorable thing to see discord preached in the pulpit, instead of the Word of God. That Luther, Melanchthon, and other Divines of the same party were true servants of the Lord to whom the Holy Spirit had imparted many gifts; but they were not infallible... Luther and Melanchthon, feeling Religion attacked on all sides would not at first startle the pople by giving them a right notion of the [Eucharist]... they expected a favorable opportunity to explain perfectly [its] nature... Luther was ignorant of many things when he began... the Reformation [which] the Lord revealed... afterwards." Corro suggested further that the early Lutherans realized their task was rather to " destroy... Antichrist that to restore the Church... purge Popery than to find out the pure truth... Hence it is that their works are full... injurious expressions." He concluded this section with an appeal to all Lutherans and Calvinists not " to make our Ministers Gods, or rather Idols, and keep our quarrels and divisions for their sake." Later he remarked that Christ's doctrines should be exalted above those of " John or Martin." His solution to the bitter sacramental hostilities was to leave to each " his liberty to follow that which God shall teach him " since the *raison d'être* behind the Eucharist was man's dullness owing to the Fall which thereafter necessitated a " visible ceremony." [79] At the same time Corro observed a simple and orthodox view of the symbolic aspect of the controversy from the Calvinist side. Other statements, such as " The true temple of Jesus Christ is... the heart of a faithful man " [80] were later reinterpreted as tending towards the deification of humanity, just as his highly individualistic, irenic counsel on the Eucharist would be seized upon to attack him, regardless of the statement's original circumstances.

It is not surprising that this document displeased even Orange,[81] who then looked to the German Lutheran princes for support, although in comparison with most Calvinist observations on Lutheranism it was hardly violent; we may take for granted the Lutherans' usual tone regarding Calvinism. Rather, it showed a naiveté about the first Protestants which failed to reflect Corro's consistently wide reading in all forms of Protestantism. Probably he felt compelled to skirt gingerly, as far as possible, the central issue dividing the major Protestant camps. Similar efforts to reduce intra-Protestant differences abound in the *Letter*, yet much of this ineffective irenicism is at once undermined by Corro's scathing analysis of Matthias Flaccius Illyricus's recent ultra-Lutheran Confession of Faith in which the Spaniard displayed his lively knowledge of the squabbles among the Lutherans to their detriment. This, in part at least, was motivated by Corro's own recent harsh experience with Flaccius who attended, and helped wreck the above-cited efforts by Pérez, et al, to achieve cooperation.

We noted Corro's pains to minimize the Eucharistic controversies which struck him as needless. He never grasped the rock-bottom importance and contemporary insolubility of this issue. Even his " safe " symbolic view of it was to lead to accusations of Zwinglianism in London in the last analysis.[82] Considering the Théobon note it is interesting that Corro included the followers of Osiander, Brenz, and Melanchthon, along with orthodox Lutherans and Calvinists in his sweeping blast at fractious sectaries who were ruining true religion.[83] In the context which produced this and like statements it is hard to see how, looking backwards, Corro shortly was branded as a ubiquitarian, Osiandrian (not to mention Servetian), and the rest. Obviously the *Letter* was carefully excerpted from in the campaign against Corro in England shortly to be analyzed. On the basis of the *Letter* the great Dutch historian, Fruin, commented: " Corro... was better fitted to heal discord; he was neither Calvinist nor Lutheran; he wanted only to be an ' Evangelical Christian.' He was less zealous for unity of doctrine than for unity in love and brotherhood. He preached the union of all Protestants against Rome, and even against Rome he would not fight maliciously. But... his influence was not to be great. His little book published at that time was only slightly disseminated, and then rarely." [84] We prefer the designation ' Evangelical Calvinist ' for this period of Corro's life; otherwise much of what Fruin observed over a century ago remains quite accurate.

On March 15, 1567 the curious *Letter to Philip II* appeared in Antwerp,[85] two days after the Osterweel disaster had ensured the Regent's triumph and the departure from the scene of persons like Corro. His motivation in composing this piece is incomprehensible. Probably it never reached the king, and even if it had its appeals for clemency for the Low Countries' Calvinists, comparison of Catholicism with Protestantism to the former's detriment, and suggestion that Philip preside over a grand all-Christian ecumenical conference with the Pope's exclusion hardly would have struck a responsive chord in the ruler who had already decided to send Alba. Theologically this second *Letter* was a companion piece to the first, and aroused similarly belated misconceptions. We have already commented on its autobiographical introduction.[86] Corro obviously left Antwerp before the entry of the Regent's army on March 27, but as he did not show up in London until April 8 he must have successfully hidden somewhere.[87]

[1] The author's forthcoming essay "Reform and Counterreform: The Case of the Spanish Heretics" will appear later in a memorial collection in honor of E. Harris Harbison, as yet unscheduled for publication by the Princeton Press. It will discuss this problem.

[2] What follows is taken largely from this work; a microfilm copy of the 1575 English version is at the University of Michigan library. It was composed and published first at Antwerp. A fruitless appeal for clemency on behalf the just-defeated rebels in particular, and for toleration generally, it also tried to appeal to Philip's independence of and occasional difficulties with the Papacy. One indication of the probable unreliability of the autobiographical section is that it is only in the later editions that Corro says he met Constantino, the leader of the Seville group after Gil's demise. Dr. McFadden makes this point well on p. 40 of his dissertation.

[3] For Reina see note 5, ch. I above; on Valera see the author's forthcoming article "A Note on the Spanish Heretic," *Hispania Sacra* 18 fasc. I (1965). On Constantino (as he is usually called) see Marcel Bataillon, *Erasme et l'Espagne* (Paris, 1937): chs. X, XIII and the unpublished PhD. thesis of William B. Jones "Constantino Ponce de la Fuente" Vanderbilt University (1964): 2 v.

[4] J. E. Longhurst, "Julián Hernández, Protestant Martyr" *Bibliothèque d'Humanisme et Renaissance* 22 (1960): p. 92f provides a recent useful summary of the case. Gil was convicted for dubiousness on a few particulars; not until after his death, in 1556, were his remains disinterred to be burned for "Lutheranism."

[5] *Ibid.*, pp. 90-118. Bullinger is not mentioned in Corro's "autobiography" in the *Letter to the King* already discussed. But in a letter to the Zuricher in 1574 he was to claim that he had read him while in San Isidro. See *PSP* 51: pp. 254-55.

[6] In Corro's case this presumably applies *before* he got to Geneva and studied at Lausanne.

[7] Americo Castro, "Lo Hispánico y el Erasmismo: *Revista de Filología hispánica* 4 (1942): p. 20. My italics.

[8] McFadden, p. 54 n 1; *GN*, 3: p. 6 f; H. C. Lea, *A History of the Inquisition in Spain* (NY. 1907) 3: p. 437 ff.

[9] Ernst Schäfer, *Geschichte des spanischen Protestanten und die Inquisition* (Gütersloh, 1902) 2: p. 355 ff.

[10] J. H. Hessels, *Ecclesiae Iondino-batavae Archivum* (Cambridge, 1897) 3 i: p. 46; *BW*, 3: p. 7. From this 1567 note of Corro's antagonist in London, Jean Cousin, we learn he went through Genoa. Some of the other known routes to Geneva from Spain were overland through the Huguenot southwest and south France, and by sea to the Low Countries and then down the Rhine valley. This same letter suggests Corro was

perhaps the first San Isidrian to meet Calvin. It should be noted here that we have to rely, and interpret, a great deal from Cousin's correspondence with respect to Corro, and the former's handwriting presented formidable obstacles, as a perusal of Hessels will show.

[11] The Juan Diaz case in 1546 sensationally demonstrated this. See most recently G. L. Pinette, " Die Spanier und Spanien im Urteil des deutschen Volkes zur Zeit der Reformation," *Archiv für Reformationsgeschichte* 48 (1957): pp. 182-91. Contemporary accounts can be found in J. Crespin, *Histoire des Martyrs* (Toulouse, 1885) I: pp. 486-87 and *RAE* 20 which indicate the furor it created.

[12] McFadden, ch. V, closely studied Corro and Lausanne at this time, incorporating archival data with secondary accounts.

[13] *Ibid.*, p. 78 ff for the Academy's typical curriculum.

[14] Henri Vuilleumier, *Histoire de l'Église réformée du Pays de Vaud sous le Régime bernois* (Lausanne, 1927) I: pp. 645-69. McFadden relies heavily on this and other works by Vuilleumier listed in his bibliography.

[15] Corro's Théobon letter of 1563, cited and discussed at length below, suggests as much.

[16] See Calvin's complimentary remarks about him in the letter of May 26, 1559 preserved in *CR* 45: columns 533-35 no. 3061. Credit for finding this source belongs to McFadden, p. 109 n 3.

[17] *Ibid.* Many years later Corro referred to it in his *Spanish Grammar*, a copy of which is on microfilm at the University of Michigan library. See also Amado Alonso, " Identificación de Gramáticos españoles clásicos," *Revista de Filología espanola* 35 (1951): pp. 231 f.

[18] Paul Geisendorf, *Theodore de Bèze* (Geneva, 1949): pp. 120 ff.

[19] See the author's article " It Pursuit of Heresy," *Historical Journal*, 9; iii (1966): pp. 275-285 for a discussion of this point.

[20] See notes 45, 46 below.

[21] McFadden, ch. VII, has summarized Corro's brief, and rather unimportant stay at Aire, collating the scanty primary and secondary data. Although then called a " college," it actually combined the equivalents of modern-day elementary and secondary schools.

[22] In the letter cited in note 16 above, and Corro's letter to Calvin of October 27, 1561, *ibid.* 46: columns 226-27 no. 3266.

[23] See note 19 above. Suffice it to note here that in addition to the religious problem Jeanne and Philip II had conflicting claims to Spanish Navarre and the Albret lands, respectively.

[24] Corro to Calvin in the letter cited in note 22 above.

[25] *Ibid.* Eduard Böhmer, " Antonio del Corro," *BSHPF* 50 (1901): pp. 202-03 notes that in the winter of 1560-1561 Corro had gone to Bordeaux carrying a message from Calvin to a colloquy being held there, which spoke well of Calvin's estimate of the bearer; Corro doubtless initiated his contacts with the Bordeaux marranos at that time. See: also M. F. Van Lennep, *De Hervorming in Spanje* (Haarlem, 1901): p. 393 n. 4.

[26] For further remarks on the pseudonym see *BW-* 3: p. 9 n 22 and *Kerk. St.* pp. 222 f.

[27] See the author's article " Marcus Pérez and Marrano Calvinism in the Dutch Revolt and the Reformation " *Bibliothèque d'Humanisme et Renaissance* 29 (1967): pp. 121-132. See also the works of Théophile Malvezin, *Histoire des Juifs à Bordeaux* (Bordeaux, 1875): pp. 69-98 and *Histoire du Commerce de Bordeaux depuis les origines jusqu'à nos jours* (Bordeaux, 1892): 2: p. 50 ff, whose antiquity suggest the need for modern research into this fascinating subject.

[28] E.g. Rachel Lopez de Villeneuve was Montaigne's mother.

[29] Malvezin, *Hist. du Commerce* 2: p. 51. As at Antwerp it seems clear the majority were sincere Catholics, as were Marcus Pérez's parents even after their son's conversion to Calvinism.

[30] In *CR* 47: colums 229-30. Dr. McFadden's indefatigable industry searched this out, and I owe my colleague, Professor Anthony Molho, a great debt of gratitude for assisting me with the Latin, and also with the Italian in the Firpo articles cited below.

[31] Toulouse, Archives municipales, BB II, Deliberations (from McFadden, p. 140 n 1).

[32] *CR* 47: p. 282 f, n°. 3114.

[33] The evidence is in Hessels 3 i: p. 33 when in March, 1564 Corro recommended De Nort's home, now in La Rochelle, as a stopping-off place for Reina.

[34] *CR* 48: column 100. See note 39 below for an extended discussion of this letter and what it revealed of Corro.

[35] Hessels, 3 i: 33; *NCF* 7: pp. 74-75.

[36] Toulouse, Archives municipales, AA 6, no. 187: p. 358 (from McFadden, p. 142 n 1).

[37] E.g. note 35 above; Bernuy's home was sacked by victorious Catholics before Monluc's army entered on May 18, 1562. See also Cl. Devic and J. Vaissete, *Histoire générale de Languedoc* (Toulouse, 1889) II: p. 390.

[38] Devic and Vaissete II: p. 385.

[39] Same as note 34 above: columns 99-100.

[40] *BW* 3: pp. 9 f.

[41] Same as note 39 above. It seems clear that the Spanish in Geneva were siding with Corro in this business. In Hessels 3 i: p. 46 we get the hostile Cousin's *ex post facto* remarks suggesting Farías's dislike of Corro; both were ex-San Isidrians and Farías was then in London. But once Corro arrived in London Farías was his staunchest Spanish ally, as we shall see below. Cf. *BW* 3: p. 7.

[42] Same as note 39 above: column 100.

[43] *Ibid.*

[44] Beza, *Epistolarum Theologicarum* (1575 ed.): pp. 259-60.

[45] Found most conveniently in *RAE* 18: pp. 59-76, in Spanish; *BW* 3: pp. 78-81 in Latin; Corro's own *Acta consistorii ecclesiae Londinogallica cum responso Antonii Corrani* (London, 1571): pp. 26-28.

[46] *Acta*, p. 25; Hessels 3 i: p. 33 which is another Corro to Reina letter at this time, but lacking the Théobon note's significance.

[47] *Acta* p. 26 (*BW* 3: pp. 83-89 contain the *Acta*).

[48] See note 5, ch. I above; in Reina's case sodomy and adultery were joined with doctrinal charges to form a rather incredible array of dubious accusations.

[49] Hessels 3 i: p. 67.

[50] *Epist. Theol.* (1575 ed.): p. 252; *Acta* pp. 26-27. A useful guide to the thought of men like these, as well as the originals in this context, is J. Lecler, *Toleration and the Reformation* (2 v. T. Westow, transl. NY, 1960).

[51] William K. Jordan, *Development of Religious Toleration in England* (Cambridge, 1932): p. 22.

[52] Hessels 3 i: p. 46; *BW* 2: p. 172.

[53] Hessels 2: p. 236-237.

[54] Same as note 48 above and Pt. II ch. 1 below.

[55] *BW* 2: p. 220.

[56] Archives historiques du Département de la Gironde 17: pp. 301-05. (from McFadden, p. 214 n 3).

[57] G. Charrier, *Les Jurades de la Ville de Bergerac tirées des registres de l'hôtel de ville* (Bergerac, 1894) 3: p. 249.

[58] To Strasbourg, Frankfurt, and Basel, specifically. See note 54 above.

[59] Archives départementales des Basses-Pyrénées, B 13, Folio 12 verso; Turin, Archivio di Stato, " Compte deuxième de Messire Jehan du Pays Trésorier et Receveur pour l'année finissant en 1565 ", folio 17

recto (from McFadden, p. 217 n 1-2) which shows Corro received the handsome pension of three hundred livres tournois annually; Pérez two hundred. The extra one hundred livres to Corro probably was for his dependents whereas Pérez, as far as is known, remained a bachelor. From *BW* 3: p. 14 n 39 we learn that Renée had heard favorable news of Corro as far back as 1561 from a Daniel Toussain, Sieur de Beaumont, then minister at Orleans. This was around the same time La Fromentée of Bordeaux was trying to undermine Corro, and once more indicates the latter's unusual range of acquaintances, even at this early period.

[60] Böhmer, " Corro ", pp. 209-10; *GN* 3: p. 175. More recently on Morel see N. Sutherland, " Calvinism and the Conspiracy of Amboise," *History* (June, 1962): pp. 118 ff.

[61] The letter was published in the *BSHPF* 30 (1881): p. 452. See also Van Lennep, pp. 353-54; *Pred.*, pp. 26-28.

[62] Pérez and Cypriano de Valera seem to have been the only reasonably well known Spanish Protestants to have escaped doctrinal and other difficulties. On Pérez see *BW* 2: pp. 55-100; *RAE* 2, 3, 7, 12, and 17 have large samplings of his numerous writings.

[63] Hessels, 3 i: p. 44.

[64] *Ibid.*, 3 i: pp. 44-45.

[65] *BSHPF*, 50 (1901): p. 212. Presumably this decision ended Renée's reluctance to part with his services; she had already released Pérez.

[66] *Ibid.*, 30 (1881): p. 457; see also Van Lennep, pp. 353 f; *Pred.*, pp. 29-31; Böhmer, " Corro ", pp. 456 f; E. Rodocanachi, *Renée de France* (Paris, 1896): p. 424 for discussions of this point.

[67] Corro's letter of July 15, 1568 discusses this; it is reprinted in F. de Schickler, *Les Églises du refuge en Angleterre* (Paris, 1892) 3: pp. 74-77.

[68] Charles Rahlenbeck, " Jean Taffin ", *BCHEW* 2 (1887): pp. 149-51 thinks that Taffin rather than Pérez promoted Corro's coming to Antwerp. Taffin was a close associate of Orange's and though a strict Calvinist saw the overriding necessity for religious amity in the Low Countries, and wanted Corro's services to further the creation of a united Protestant front; Pérez, of course, worked along the same line and there is no reason to think both men did not press Corro to come. See also the same author's *L'Inquisition et la Réforme en Belgique* (Brussels, 1857): p. 99 and Van Lennep, p. 395. More recently for Taffin, and Villiers, see C. Boer, *Hofpredikers van Prins Willem van Oranje* (S'Gravenhague, 1952). On Corro's refusal to sign the Confession see *BW* 3: p. 19 and Hessels 3 i: p. 51 which discloses an attempt to imply Corro's ministerial role in Antwerp was irregular as to his election.

[69] See note 27 above.

[70] *AA* II: pp. 154-56.

[71] *Ibid.*, 11: p. 180; B. van den Brink, et al, *Correspondance de Marguerite de Parme avec Philippe II* (Utrecht, 1925-42) I: p. 232; *La defense de Messire Antoine de Lalaing, Comte de Hocstrate... d'après l'édition originale de 1568 augmentée de la correspondance inédite du Comte... avec Marguerite de Parme...* (Mons, 1837): pp. 117 ff.

[72] *AA* 11: pp. 151-52.

[73] *GN* 3: p. 108; Edmond Poullet and Charles Piot, *Correspondance du Cardinal Granvelle* (Brussels, 1877-96) 2: p. 158; *AA* 11: pp. 151-52.

[74] Same as note 71 above.

[75] *La défense de... Hocstrate*, pp. 129-30; his other comments on Corro and allied matters are in *AA* 11: pp. 164-65, 172, 180-81, and 198-99.

[76] Same as note 74 above, and Brussels, Archives générales du Royaume, Fonds: Papiers d'État et d'Audience, no. 261 folio 192 (from McFadden, p. 275 n 1).

[77] See note 69 above.

[78] This excerpt is taken from the English translation of G. Brandt, *History of the Reformation in the Low Countries* (Michael de la Roche, transl., London, 1725) 1: pp. 109-10. McFadden lists all and extant editions on pp. 757-59, and these are followed, it is appropriate to note here by similar listings of Corro's other works from pp. 759-72. As with note 2 above the University of Michigan library has a useful microfilm copy which we have consulted.

[79] Univ. of Mich. microfilm no 11918 (case 35, carton 207, short-title catalog 5787): section 21 Bv recto to verso (original pagination).

[80] *Ibid.*, section 24 Bv recto to verso.

[81] The evidence, however, comes again from the doubtful pen of Cousin in Hessels 3 i: p. 51, and was written later in the spring of 1567 in a letter to the Antwerpers as part of the campaign discussed below to discredit Corro on the continent shortly after he arrived in London in April.

[82] Elsewhere he seemed to recommend the individual's right to interpret it; e.g. Univ. of Mich. microfilm, section 18 Bv recto to verso where as to the Lord's Supper Corro allows "everyone his liberty to follow that which God shall teach him." See note 5 above for other data pointing towards a possible Zwinglianism on Corro's part.

[83] *Ibid.*, section 24 Bv recto to verso; section 79 Fj recto to verso in particular as well as Corro's introductory "prayer for concord of doctrine." The *Letter to the King*, appearing shortly after expressed similar sentiments.

[84] R. Fruin, " Het Voorspel van den Tachtigjarigen Oorlog," *De Gids* (New Series, 1859-60) 2 i: pp. 417-18 (reprinted in Fruin's *Verspreide Geschriften* (S'Gravenhague, 1900) 1: pp. 266-449).

[85] See note 78 above for McFadden's comprehensive listings; also Univ. of Mich. microfilm no. 11918 (case 35, carton 953, short-title catalog 5791).

[86] See note 2 above.

[87] Hessels 3 i: pp. 48, 51; *Polem.*, p. 9 and *GN* 3: pp. 95-96, 102-03 where Sepp suggests he preached to Orange at Breda, and also briefly was in France after the Osterweel debacle. His evidence is weak.

III. IN ENGLAND (1567 - 1591)

I. CONTROVERSIES WITH THE STRANGERS' CHURCHES
(1567-1570)

Virtually from the moment he set foot in Elizabeth's England Corro was involved in debates and controversies which rapidly increased in acrimony and complexity.[1] Not surprisingly he had hoped to reconstitute the Spanish Calvinist congregation which had foundered in the wake of Reina's flight, and whose members now were divided chiefly between the French and Italian Strangers' Churches.[2] Consequently during April 11-13 Corro conferred with three prominent refugees who had been involved in the affairs of that earlier church with a view towards a new unity. Two, Balthazar Sánchez and Angelin Victorius, had been Reina's violent opponents, while the third, Francisco Farías, another former San Isidrian, had backed him.[3] The cohesion characterizing the marranos of Bordeaux did not exist among the London Spanish, and Corro sought an outlet for his preaching intentions in the French Church.

Immediately the Théobon letter with its suspect queries and remarks was brought to public view, and various personages on the continent were asked opinions of Corro.[4] Pastor Cousin and the elders wondered why Corro had " meddled with writers who bad doctrines are known." [5] Given Corro's previously described attitude about this kind of reading such a question revealed at once the impassable gulf between him and his interlocutors, and augured poorly for the future. Corro was never one to await an outcome idly; he presented himself before the Consistory replete with testimonials from Montargis and Antwerp. It spoke volumes for both parties that the French dismissed the former because it was too eulogistic and therefore possibly not genuine, and suspected the latter because its seals had been tampered with.[6] In view of Renée's treatment of Corro and her reluctance to lose his services the French clearly were acting too sensitively about the whole business, but one can appreciate their apprehensiveness over the broken seals. On the other hand in their letters of inquiry about Corro to Des Gallars and the Church of Paris they enclosed a French version of the Théobon note which omitted the important sections in which the Spaniard discussed the projected Castilian Bible and which showed his obviously excellent relations with Jeanne d'Albret.[7] Considering all this it hardly surprises one that relations deteriorated speedily between Corro and the leaders of the London French. Apparently Corro attended services at their church erratically during this time, and while the Consistory felt him liable to its jurisdiction and discipline he had other ideas since he was denied the pulpit. This impasse arrived at, the matter was referred to a commission presided over by Edmund Grindal, Bishop of London, for judgment. From what followed we think Corro insisted on this appeal rather than the French.[8]

On June 5, 1567 the commission presented a formal statement signed by Grindal to the French, the salient points of which were that on examination by " pious and learned men " it had been deemed Corro was " averse [sic !] from all impious positions " and favored the doctrine and gospel " which our own and other reformed churches profess." Grindal added that he hoped Corro would prove as satisfactory to all others as he had shown himself to be to him.[9] Among Corro's successful points of defense were his claims that the strictly private, between-theologians nature of the Théobon letter should have been honored from the first, and the related one that as a theologian he had every right to ask questions and read materials where he would without being presumed a follower of one or another of the relevant sects. That such arguments carried greater weight in Elizabethan England than with Calvinist communities is scarcely novel. Shortly afterwards the disappointed Cousin wrote that Corro had actually confessed to Grindal his inability to sustain the controversial sentences of the famous letter, but this appears preposterous in view of the above-cited wording of the June 5 decision, and as it occurred in a letter sent to François Hotman at Bourges it probably can be interpreted as a deliberate misstatement, designed to malign Corro abroad.[10] Nor was this kind of tactic restricted to private correspondence.

Despite his jurisdictional powers over the refugee congregations Grindal rarely interfered directly with them, which is another reason for believing Corro initiated the appeal to him rather then French. For reasons not at all clear he did not follow up his triumph by formally joining the French Church and preaching there; perhaps he realized the Consistory's solidarity against him would have made working there very difficult, nor is it altogether implausible to suggest that Grindal cautioned him about stirring matters further by publicizing his vindication in quite that way. The other bloc of Spaniards in London belonged to the Italian Church, as previously noted, and possibly at Grindal's urging, Corro joined it, and subsequently preached occasionally to that congregation as a whole. When Cousin wrote Hotman on June 16 he praised the deity " for delivering us from such a man "[11]; presumably this referred to Corro's enrollment in the other church. The French, however, could not ignore his galling presence in the refugee community as a whole, and by July 18 the well-meaning Grindal was compelled to inform Cousin that Corro had complained of his Church's constant efforts to label him as a " Servetian " in the eyes of the local Calvinist exiles.[12] It does not seem that the French took any trouble to appease Grindal, much less Corro, at this time. Pretty clearly they knew their bishop.

From the mid-July exchange of notes between Cousin and Grindal[13] we learn also that a minority of the French congregation, undoubtedly its Spanish members, had been agitating to hear Corro preach. While this must have disturbed Cousin and his associates greatly Grindal acknowledged having refused to support their demand. One is reminded somewhat of the Bordeaux situation, and indeed throughout his London squabbles with the French Corro found their fear of losing members a powerful element in their antipathy towards him. Early in September the Sixth National Synod of the Reformed Churches of France met at Vertueil, and added a new, acerbic note to the situation in London by excluding Corro from the ministry until he had cleared himself of the charges stemming from the Théobon note.[14] To suggest Corro saw behind this pronouncement the continuing activity of the London French is barely necessary to observe at this juncture. It is distinctly possible they were in collusion with the aforementioned, and greatly biased Morel in this matter, although this cannot be proved. The Vertueil statement directly contravened the June 5 decision by Grindal and his colleagues, but nothing indicates any distress on the latter's part with respect to the proceedings at Vertueil. But with the June 5 favorable verdict behind him Corro let it be known he was considering publishing a formal " Apology " in his defence which would expose his enemies' machinations and distortions, although he must have been aware of Grindal's continuing policy of non-interference just reiterated by his silence in face of what in some respects could be construed as the negation of his authority and judgment concerning the Calvinist refugees of London. Presumably under some pressure Corro failed to print the " Apology " while the certificate of orthodoxy of June 5 failed also to obtain sufficient circulation; thus Corro was to be effectively prevented from getting the kind of impressive support, from persons such as the Colignys, Renée of Ferrara, and Jeanne d'Albret, which would have stood him very well in the aftermath. These, in turn, were constrained to keep silent if indeed they were not persuaded of his " guilt " by such pronouncements as those emanating from Vertueil. His opponents subsequently had the field to themselves with respect to the continent.

On December 8 Cousin met with four of his ministerial colleagues to discuss the Corro affair in view of the Spaniard's threats revolving around the proposed " Apology." [15] This was without appreciable effect on matters, and the French apparently failed to connect Corro's silence in print with Grindal's attitudes. But if Corro felt the time inexpedient for frontal attack on the French he was not merely biding his time in frustration. In the months since his landing in England he had somehow managed to cultivate relations with several of the great leaders of the country, which were to stand him in very good stead hereafter.[16] The first concrete evidence of such a contact was his January 16, 1568 letter to Matthew Parker, Archbishop of Centerbury, which accompanied French editions of his two Antwerp publications, purportedly sent to aid Parker's sons in their study of that language.[27] In the course of relating various matters of common interest Corro noted that he had been receiving a quarterly allowance from Grindal, which adds further to the already considerable complexity of the relationship between the two. The Spaniard lays his services before the Archbishop and the " realm ", which suggests he already viewed England as his permanent home. Without the kind of connections he had been obtaining Corro probably would not have commented thusly to Parker. As we shall see he maintained excellent relations with the primate of England, and Parker for one never condemned any of Corro's writings which came to his notice. The fact that from the first Parker found nothing theologically offensive in the Antwerp *Letters*, both of which contained generous samples of Corró's doctrines then under fire from Calvinists like Beza and Cousin suggests further the extreme and often scarcely justifiable reactions of the latter group to even the remotest hint of heterodoxy. In this case we believe that personalities and circumstances played the determinant roles despite doctrinal appearances.

In the interim Corro carried on his work with the Spanish members of the Italian Church with the full approval of its leader, Pastor Jerlito, and the Consistory, which, so far, had taken no notice of his quarrels with the French. The Italians must have known the substance of the charges against him but apparently the June 5 decision satisfied them.[18] Corro's residence at this time underlines his range of influential acquaintances. His landlady in the Cripplegate Ward tenement was the Duchess of Suffolk.[19] Typically enough Cousin complained to Grindal that Corro was preaching in French to tempt the Spaniards in his own church to join the Italian congregation, which accusation ignited another bitter round between the two.[20]

Early in the summer of 1568 Corro made up for not having followed through his previous threat to publish the aforementioned "Apology." He had printed and circulated throughout London a pamphlet composed of English and French versions of Grindal's June 5 verdict prefaced by his own blast at the French for opening his correspondence and refusing him a copy of the Théobon letter.[21] On July 15 he penned a long letter to Grindal in which for the first time he compared his accusers with the infamous Spanish Inquisition.[22] He specifically charged Cousin with having "suborned" eminent persons like Des Gallars against him, which process had resulted in his calumniation at the recent Synods of Vertueil and Angoumois. Balthazar Sánchez, so effective in the campaign against Reina, had been sent by the London French to Angoumois solely to hurry proceedings against Corro, who suggested that using a man such as Sánchez merely disguised flimsily the anti-Spanish attitude of the French who saw a Servetian lurking in every Spaniard. In fact, there was some substance to Corro's remark, as the future demonstrated. As a man who had fled at great peril Spain, the Inquisition, and the Papacy (so to speak) Corro clearly felt he deserved different treatment from Calvinists. He resented being labelled a Lutheran and a Servetian, as the inspiration seemed to strike his accusers, regardless of the bases of such opposed charges. Grindal's feelings about this impassioned, verbose letter remain unknown, but considering his definite turn against Corro shortly thereafter we are right to think he found it offensive.[23] Since he had as little sympathy for Calvinist-style organization and discipline as Corro the latter's attacks in that sector could not have been disturbing, although the intemperate bracketing of the National Synods with the Spanish Inquisition may have ruffled the peaceable Bishop's sense of Protestant honor. Rather, however, given exactly his inclinations away from strife in this whole matter, as shown by his consistent attitude of standing above the battle once the June 5 decision had been rendered, he probably felt that Corro was verging on reopening it all over again. That was the last thing Edmund Grindal wanted, even if the June 5 verdict had failed of its peace-making purpose, as Vertueil clearly proved. On July 22 the French Consistory protested vehemently to Grindal about the aforementioned pamphlet which Corro himself had apparently handed to an unnamed member of the church the day before.[24] The Spaniard, probably assuming support from his well-placed English friends, had, as it turned out, momentarily overreached himself by this tactless gesture. In the ensuing trying months he was quite bereft of direct assistance from on high.

On August 27 Cousin told Grindal about Corro's supposed preaching in French, previously noted. Grindal presumably conveyed this latest complaint to him for on August 31 Corro wrote the Consistory defending himself and, curiously, insinuated that Cousin lacked its unanimous backing.[25] This, of course, must have been a calculated stab in the dark to sow dissension in the ranks, which missed its mark in the immediate aftermath. Two days later the irritated Consistory asked the harassed Grindal for a copy of Corro's July 15 letter to him and requested protection from the fiery Spaniard's " libels." [26] For the good Bishop's edification they enclosed Corro's August 31 note. Meanwhile Corro was appealing for justice to his old schoolmaster, Theodore Beza, now Calvin's successor at Geneva.[27] We can only surmise that Corro believed a favorable statement from there would easily override the London French and their continental allies, and in conjunction with the June 5 judgment and the one of July 23, 1563 indicated in Merlin's letter to Calvin, would permanently vindicate him and put a firm conclusion to his recent difficulties. Above all the obstacles to his evangelizing work among Spaniards would be removed. The very friendly tone of this letter reveals that Corro was still unaware how badly disposed Beza had become towards him; that time was in the offing, and would entail the end of his deep reverence for Geneva and Calvin's successor as the founts of objective authority. For the time being Beza failed to respond while the London French drew up a new list of charges against Corro, presumably at Grindal's request, or at least with his subsequent approval. *Les Articles que l'Eglise Francoise met en auant contre Antoine Corran Espagnol* were presented to the Bishop on November 28, 1568, and were subdivided into four basic sections: ambition, calumnies, lies, and scurrility.[28] These are illustrated by excerpts from the accused's printed works and from replies to earlier requests from abroad noted before. Thirteen signatures were appended to the French and Latin copies.

Some summarizing of these charges will give the reader a fair idea of the kind of infighting this contemporary source shows. Under ambition, which seems to have been one of the consistent complaints against Corro throughout his career, the French said he had threatened to return to France (which makes very little sense since Montargis was not mentioned in such a context; where else could he go unless the Béarn?), and they delve more fully into the question of jurisdiction over him. It is stated categorically that just after Corro's arrival in London the Antwerp Consistory had discharged him from ministry, but no available evidence sustains this.[29] Further he had supported the faction in their church which had wanted him as a preacher, which even if directly true is hardly surprising. Little of this strikes us as ambition *per se*. But almost certainly the root of this discord lies here. Corro rejected their claims to supervision while pressing for the creation of a Spanish conventicle within their congregation. The matter was irreconcilable, and the loosely bandied charges and countercharges turned on this without ever coming to grips with it. As we shall see shortly the Fulham verdict a few months later rendered a draconian solution.

Among Corro's calumnies was his supposed declaration that he would have received greater hospitality from heathens and infidels, which aroused the sensibilities of the French who replied that one of their elders had indeed cared for him on his arrival. This descent into pettiness was not atypical. They denied his charge that they conspired with the two Spanish associates of Juan Pérez against him, and implied that he had been maligning respected individuals, including fellow Spaniards. A very feeble defence of their interception of his correspondence was included in this section.[30] His chief lie which had upset them had been Corro's charge of procrastination on their part during the winter of 1567-8 when he had sought the good offices of four French clergy in order to resolve peacefully the issues between himself and the Consistory. The absence of other data prevents us from analyzing this reference. Under scurrilities, which seem to have been taken from the pamphlet distributed earlier that year by Corro, and which has already been described, they listed his jeers and lampoons against themselves and their church. The original is worth excerpting from:

" Les brocars de Corran sont en grand nombre en quoy il monstre qu'il est bien versé en l'art de moquerie..." [31]

Although a paragraph implied Corro's " Servetianism ", inasmuch as it suggested he denied Christ's humanity (which, in fact, was the direct opposite of the usual implication in his Christology), and also attacked the irenicism, real and imagined of the *Letter to the Lutheran Ministers...*, the burden of these accusations was personal, even petty. Some truth existed among them; on the other hand the belated references to the *Letter* and Christology suggest the French themselves recognized the need to buttress their other accusations with something more solid, even if more or less by innuendo. Grindal probably was taken aback by Corro's apparent talents in " the art of mockery." He showed the document to Corro almost immediately, but also followed his opponents' request for a new commission to reinvestigate the Spaniard, and in particular to use the advice of some twenty-odd Calvinist ministers recently arrived from France.[32]

The Bishop constituted a new committee from six of these exiled French pastors and an undetermined number from the Royal Ecclesiastical Commission. Among the former was Pierre Loiseleur de Villiers, who from this time would play a prominent role in Corro's life. Corro may have felt a bit optimistic about the outcome of this new deliberation on hearing that Laurent Bourguignon was on the committee; he was presently chaplain to Cardinal Châtillon, one of Corro's influential acquaintances from Montargis days, now in England. Three eminent Anglicans involved were Gabriel Goodman, Dean of Westminister, Thomas Huick, Grindal's Vicar General in Spirituals, and William Bedell,

Clerk of the Ecclesiastical Commissioners. Since Corro had been a preaching member of the Italian Church of London for so long it is striking that no one represented it on this committee.

While there is no extant record of the Anglo-French committee's sittings it is clear that it reached its verdict on March 17, 1569 only after a very conscientious searching of Corro and his enemies.[33] Read aloud by Grindal at the Fulham episcopal palace the committee's conclusion was that Corro was guilty of evil speaking, slander, and obstinacy, and therefore he was suspended from any ministerial functions and forbidden to preach, read, and interpret the word of God.[34] Nowhere in the document were doctrinal offences touched on; Corro's consistent defence of the inviolable privacy of his correspondence and right to read where he would in that connection had proved successful. However, in view of his intemperate outbursts at these proceedings, such as his notorious explosion: " It is evident that Englishmen do not only wage civil wars against the Spaniards, but ecclesiastical also; civil in taking their ships and money, ecclesiastical in my person ",[35] the adverse judgment on the personal charges comes as no surprise. Under the circumstances Corro's foolish allusion to the English government's recent illegal detention and confiscation of Spanish pay-ships at Dover guaranteed the committee's ratification of French grievances on this score. One assumes he broke under fairly severe questioning, which cannot excuse his stupidity in this regard, however provoked. In a sense, even with six irreproachably orthodox Calvinists present Corro had triumphed. Despite the revocation of his preaching and the rest, the earlier affirmations of his doctrinal correctness had been renewed. And, as time showed, the sustenance of these personal charges was not to prove a serious road-block in his career, although that was to take very different directions. Above all the Fulham verdict by no means cost him the esteem and support of his influential lay friends, such as Cecil and Leicester, despite his violent decrying of their country's piratical policy towards Spain. Obviously they chose to ignore this, putting it down to the temporary loss of aplomb which

Grindal himself suggested as a factor here, despite his growing distaste for Corro. Corro clearly had attributes quite attractive to several of the key figures in the Government.

Just before the Fulham decision Beza took a belated hand in the quarrel between Corro and the London French which demonstrated his permanent hostility to the Spaniard. Since these letters to Grindal and Cousin were dated March 8, 1569 they never could have arrived in time to sway the committee.[36] To the former Beza sent with his letter an open statement he promised to send Corro, and all the documents the latter had been sending him to prove his innocence. While Beza told Cousin to submit to the forthcoming judgment, he also reserved his own opinion about the opening of Corro's letters to Reina as well as the misleading translations and omissions from the Théobon note already described. However, he maintained his suspicions of Corro's orthodoxy based precisely on statements made in that same letter (the Théobon one), and suggested to Grindal that he get together with Cousin to compare adverse notes. Cousin, he said, could be in error but not bad faith, which presumably was not Corro's case. In fact, Corro had initially aroused his laughter, then his anger as matters progressed. Much later Corro got to see Beza's " open letter " to him which, among other things, denied that Cousin had ever worked covertly to discredit him on the continent, and Beza said he greatly regretted Corro's intemperance in the affair. Corro must have placed a somewhat differing interpretation on Cousin's distorted letters of request to people like Des Gallars. Beza went on to attack vitriolically Spanish theology in general, sweeping Juan Valdés, Loyola, and Servetus under one rug. The fires of Seville and Valladolid were forgotten for the nonce. Such a view must have infuriated Corro; to be bracketed with a Loyola, however carelessly, must have been a bit much for him. To Corro this comment starkly revealed the total incomprehension of his situation, and that of Spanish religious refugees generally, existing at Geneva; therefore no hope of redemption was possible from that quarter. Despite the Fulham ruling the now silenced Corro was permitted to remain a communicant at the Italian Church, which so far had played a totally passive role in the proceedings. There is nothing about him in the records for the spring and early summer of 1569. But while he was not " preaching " God's word he was "reading" and "interpreting" it, the March 17 prohibition notwithstanding.

On July 15, 1569 Corro's immediately controversial *Tableau de l'Œuvre de Dieu* appeared from the press of a Flemish refugee in Norwich.[37] According to its author it had been inspired by a similar piece done in 1556 which has never been traced, and which Corro said be came across during his Antwerp days. His manuscript revision of the original had circulated among his friends there, and one of the wealthier had financed the publication of the finished product at Norwich. Corro added that the printer had asked De la Forest, minister of the French refugee church in that city, the largest in England after the London community, to proofread his work with an eye towards correctness in the French. The Calvinist minister fund the *Tableau* rife with attacks on orthodox Christology and predestination. Specifically Corro claimed that Christ was sent through the sacraments as an example to man, and he restricted the communication of the Holy Spirit to Christ when the latter had already " mounted to the heavens." [38] There is little doubt that in this work Corro did indeed pass " over the doctrine [of predestination]... only incidentally referring to [it], observing a more significant silence on... the Trinity " while stressing Christ as " true son of God and true man." [39] Our own reading of the *Tableau* leads us to believe that Corro certainly watered down the contemporary Calvinist view of election, especially reprobation. However, it took a considerable imagination or bias to read into this work as much as was by De la Forest and others. The archivist who collected most of the documents pertaining to Corro remarked that because of the *Tableau* Corro again " was accused of heresy, but it is not clear what he was charged with though it may be suspected that it was the absence of any appeal to a [specific or authorized] Confession and a Catechism." It is relevant to note from the same page of this source the observation on Beza's role in Corro's affairs on the eve of the Fulham decision: " from none of the letters [from Beza to Grindal, et al] does it appear what the disputes had really been about..." [40]

It seems plausible to think De la Forest knew of Corro's enmity to his colleagues in London. The printer's request for help with the *Tableau* must have been a marvelous, heaven-sent opportunity for him to reinforce the Fulham verdict with " proof " of doctrinal errors. De la Forest was merely doing his duty by his brethren, and the *Tableau* does document for the first time the Spaniard's wavering belief in election, although he blandly assents to it as a very general article of faith. Given Corro's life, and the tendency of Spaniards generally to take a high view of their individuality, it is not surprising that for those affected by the Reformation, with ideas as far apart as those of Servetus and Juan Pérez, the doctrine of predestination, and reprobation in particular, proved exceedingly hard to digest. None of this, however, was to bother Corro's Anglican acquaintances, most of whom despite a frequent Calvinist overlay in their religion, were not satisfied with Beza's supralapsarianism and the like, from which Corro revolted with growing explicitness from the time of the *Tableau*.

Shortly after its appearance Corro re-engaged the French in an attempt to reconcile matters, but beyond admitting his occasional brutishness of manner he would not go.[41] In view of subsequent events we think this unexpected tactic was suggested to Corro by some of his highly-placed friends, although proof is lacking. Since he still adhered to the Italian Church this comparatively olive-branch approach to the French was odd, on the face of it. The reply was a demand for retractions of old statements, such as the one bracketing them with the Inquisition. Corro rebutted this, noting in passing their refusal to admit his wife to services.[42] There seems no doubt he was baiting the French, and must have expected their reactions, which in turn presupposes the deliberateness of Corro's approach. It is thus very unlikely he was not prompted. On September 8 the French wrote him requesting his signature to their document, and noted they were going to refer his countercharges to the Bishop of London.[43] Corro had, in fact, successfully reopened his case, while at this same time Grindal was under pressure from Cecil to settle it for once and for all— preferably in Corro's favor.

The September 8 demand impelled Corro to appeal directly to Cecil, who in turn wrote Grindal on the former's behalf. On September 20 the Bishop replied to the Secretary.[44] From this we learn that Cecil had not merely asked for a termination to the entire controversy, but the restoration of Corro to his ministerial functions. Grindal recapitulated the affair since its inception and obsequiously remarked that " if anything be offered to Corro on my part that is too hard, I am well contented to refer the moderation thereof to your judgment," which was a curious commentary on relations between the leading laity and clergy. Of course, when an issue was deeply felt Grindal could say and do quite otherwise as his later years showed. He added that while he admired the Spaniard's learning he disliked his " spirit " and " dealings " and promised to send Cecil additional material so that the latter could adequately form his own opinion.[45] Grindal then turned to matters where he was on firmer grounds, and would not have to " refer the moderation... to your judgment." He observed that the Italians were now distressed over the *Tableau* and were for the first time also disquieted about Corro. The Bishop pronounced that " if the controversy with the French (which is only about offence in manners) be compounded, I cannot see but his restitution to reading or preaching must be deferred, till he... cleared himself before the governors of his own church in... doctrine, which is... of far greater moment." Not a word on Corro's breaking the Fulham prohibition about " interpreting," although he doubtless looked upon the *Tableau*'s publication merely as the formal appearance of an earlier effort, however belatedly. Cecil followed this with a reiteration of his admiration of Corro's learning, and broadly hinted at the overharshness of the terms imposed upon him at Fulham. He again urged a speedy conclusion, to which Grindal must have assented with a weary amen by now [46] Shortly afterwards he persuaded Corro to sign a brief statement retracting his comparison of the French Consistory with the Inquisition, and which gave his promise to live in peace with them; two months later Grindal sent this to Cousin,[47] by which time Corro was again a center of controversy.

Coincident with the renewal of " relations " with the French came difficulties with the Italians, alluded to by Grindal in his September 20 letter to Cecil. Early in September, 1569 their Consistory informed Corro of their intent to write out their objections to the *Tableau*, and it was mutually agreed he would respond in writing.[48] Corro's own account discloses he had already composed a reply to De la Forest's critique at this time and two Flemings accusing him before the Italians of heretical statements in the *Tableau* had refused to read it.[49] Two other Flemish members of this church then presented Corro with Jerlito's written objections and later in the fall the Spaniard prepared a very lengthy *Apologia* on the subject.[50] To the Italians' complaints that its enormity made it difficult to use expeditiously he brought forth an abridgement, called the *Responsum*.[51] He did not hide his growing disdain of orthodox predestination in these documents, although he stood fast against the other kinds of doctrinal charges.[52] But on that alone he lost the hitherto consistent good-will of the Italians and so thrust his fortunes increasingly into the hands of his English friends. Perhaps a recent and acute paraphrasal of the doctrines of Sebastian Castellion, certain of whose works Corro admired tremendously, as will be seen, suffices also to summarize the core of the Spaniard's theology: " Like Luther Castellion relied on justification by faith but with Erasmus he left a place for free will and rebelled against predestination, erected into a dogma by Calvin [and Beza]. God... wants the faith of all; a sincere spirit will always respond to grace. This allows man to raise himself through his actions above his weaknesses and natural penchant for sin; whomever has a living faith and believes with all his heart in the saving virtue of Christ becomes capable of obeying the divine laws in all matters." [53] In the 1569 defence of his *Tableau* Corro remarked that salvation was available to all through a faith which manifested itself in good works and obedience to God's will; acquisition of faith came first, however, and not through works. The possibility of an ethically-oriented religion was inherent in such an approach even if Corro did not quite intend it. In his accustomed brusque fashion he made certain of wounding even the Italians when he suggested that they repeated mindlessly predestinarian formulae whose purport they neither understood nor really believed.[55]

Throughout the fall of 1569 Corro waited patiently for the French to respond to the document Grindal had had him sign retracting his injurious comparison of them with the Inquisition. Apparently he finally learned that they had yet to receive it, and on November 4 he wrote Cecil about this.[56] He literally begged the Secretary to write Grindal on his behalf in order to put an end to his lengthy and unjustified " infamy " which was increasingly ruining his reputation abroad, according to reports from three of his friends. He did not accuse the Bishop of withholding the relevant statement but said frankly that he believed Grindal's design was to justify the Fulham verdict as much as pacify Corro himself. He also suggests Cecil write " Monsieur le Doyen ", whom McFadden took to be the previously-noticed Dean Goodman of Westminister, a member of the Fulham committee. Whether or not he was referring to Goodman the suggestion reveals Corro knew of Grindal's disenchantment with him as the Italians joined the French over the *Tableau*; this holds true despite passing references for form's sake to the Bishop's " good will " towards the Spaniard. In sum we simply do not know why Grindal delayed so long in transmitting Corro's semi-apology to the French, but once Corro discovered this he took steps to bring Cecil, and through him, others to bear on Grindal to expedite the matter. In fact, the chief impression one derives from all this is Corro's complete trust in the all-powerful Secretary, soon to be Lord Burghley. He could not have chosen a better patron as he went about burning his Calvinist bridges.

Three days later Grindal wrote Cousin, enclosing the note just discussed.[57] In asking the French minister to give him his reactions to Corro's apparent adhesion to compromise he reminded Cousin that Corro had been suspended solely for personal offences, and asked for leniency in view of the Spaniard's new attempt to heal the breach. However, he also observed that the condemnation of conduct rather than doctrine had not been " a small one ", which reenforces Corro's remark to Cecil that he was still at pains to sustain the Fulham judgment. He also told

Cousin in this letter that unless Corro were cleared of objections to the *Tableau* he could never be reinstated as described. Grindal attributed his delay in sending this out to an outbreak of plague which had caused a death in Cousin's household. It is hard, however, to avoid feeling that he was rather responding to very recent pressure from Cecil. Cousin and his Consistory moved quickly after this prod and on November 22 Grindal was informed of their willingness to end the controversy if Corro would satisfy them on personal and doctrinal grounds.[58] From Corro's position they were ignoring his September apology which should have taken care of the personal side of things, and in a sense they were insulting Grindal given their obvious inattention to his injuction about leniency in his November 7 letter to Cousin. Considering the Fulham decision they had no business reopening doctrinal matters, and strictly speaking, the *Tableau* problem belonged to the Italians who had initiated its discussion in London circles, apparently independently of De la Forest. A statement was enclosed by the French in their reply to Grindal which Corro would have to sign and which would then be read to the congregation. He was to agree to the " scandalous and imprudent " nature of the Théobon note and their correctness in having opened it, as well as the theological unsoundness of parts of the *Letter to the Lutheran Ministers* . . . which they claimed to be derogatory to the leaders of Calvinsim. He would also accept orthodox Christology and retract all of his infamous, notorious remarks about themselves. The Consistory hardly could have expected Corro to accede to such a statement, even if it had waived its humiliating suggestion it be read aloud to the assembly. The great nineteenth century scholar of Spanish Protestantism, Eduard Böhmer, observed of this episode that the London French were acting " invincibly obstinate." [59]   That was undeniable. Corro scarcely could accept the repudiation of almost his entire past which was so explicity laid out here. But the Calvinists could not be expected to make allowances for a man had who aroused Beza's ire, Grindal's distrust, and their own sustained suspicions, regardless of the course of events and their own often weak justification. In the last analysis Corro's peculiar ability to inflame matters by his personal style of writing and action, his close friendship with Reina, never remotely denied or repudiated, and his recent forthright denigrations of orthodox predestinarianism combined to ensure that they would never give the proverbial inch, Cecil and others notwithstanding. But it is a striking testimonial to Corro's connections, and resiliency, that within three weeks of this debacle a licensed English translation of his *Letter to the Lutheran Ministers...* appeared in London, translated by a Sir Geoffrey Fenton. It was reprinted the following year, and again in 1577 combined with an English version of the *Letter to the King*. Since to some extent Corro and his family depended on outright charity for sustenance during the dark years of 1569-71 [60] these authorized publications are a sharp reminder of the official favor shown his efforts, as well as an indication of the unease in relations between the English and their refugee Calvinists. During this same troubled period Corro issued a Latin version of the *Tableau* expressedly for Archbishop Parker and the Queen herself.[61]

Matters at the Italian Church came to a head by January 7, 1570 when Corro, in the congregation's presence, was admonished for his " silliness, lies, disobedience, obstinacy, and contempt for church discipline." [62] The session culminated in the exclusion of the recalcitrant from communion. Although there is no evidence of French prompting in all this Böhmer believed Corro's old antagonists had " instigated " the Italians against Corro.[63] Certainly there seems no direct connection between their reservation about the *Tableau* expressed previously and disciplinary, non-doctrinal character of the statement a few months later dismissing Corro from the congregation. In fact, around this same time the pastor of the London Dutch Church, Joris Wijbo (also called Sylvanus), was asked his opinion of the *Tableau* with the undoubted purpose of presenting the Bishop of London with a united hostile view of that piece from all the Strangers' Churches of the capitol. Wijbo, however, disappointed with his vague discussion of the *Tableau* in which he appeared mildly distressed only at Corro's occasional tendency to overemphasize human action with respect to salvation. Indeed, he suggested a special Consistory representing the three major refugee churches meet to forgive the Spaniard and bring him back among the faithful through such charity. Wijbo added that his current poor health probably prevented him from delving perhaps as deeply into this affair as he should have. Despite such modest qualifications his opinions were not received with enthusiasm by his colleagues in the refugee congregations.[64]

Corro had appealed the January 7 ruling and initially consented to its review by a panel of eleven ministers—seven Italians, two French, and two Anglicans—on January 30; one of each from the latter two groups had been on the Fulham committee.[65] But he had second thoughts and on the morrow rejected in advance any decision forthcoming from this panel since its Italian members had been among his accusers in that Church. But the new committee ignored this and went on to sustain Corro's exclusion from communion.[66] While Corro's reservations about mixing one's judges with one's prosecutors has perhaps an appealing modern ring most of his contemporaries thought otherwise, and his rapid tactical shifts were not calculated to give them much confidence in the consistency of his ideals, at least in this particular situation. One gets the distinct feeling that Corro no longer cared what the Calvinists, Italian or French, had decided, especially since the attitude towards him the French had revealed back on November 22, 1569 when they had rejected his peace-offering through Grindal. In fact, it was virtually on the eve of his condemnation by the Italians that he confidentally offered his Latin *Tableau* to the Queen, as well as a French edition. He was moving steadily towards formal adherence to Anglicanism. For the nonce he belonged to no church.[67]

On May I, 1570 Edmund Grindal was promoted to the see of York and replaced by Edwin Sandys, a close associate of William Cecil and the Earl of Leicester. The significance of this change of supervisors of refugee affairs in London can best be appreciated by citing the rather awkward but accurate phrases of the editor of *Grindal's Remains*: " At length, by the favor chiefly of... Leicester, but not before Grindal was removed to York, Corro broke through the clouds." [68]

2. CONCLUSION OF CONTROVERSIES WITH THE STRANGERS' CHURCHES THROUGH THE TEMPLE CHURCH READERSHIPS AT THE INNS OF COURT (1570 - 1576)

Grindal's translation to York coincided with the French Church's direct entry into the *Tableau* controversy. One of Corro's judges at Fulham, Villiers, joined the Italians and Pastor De la Forest of Norwich in condemning the tract, and Corro at once protested. Another six-man panel of Frenchmen was rapidly organized, and Corro and Villiers debated over the *Tableau* in its presence.[69] In the course of upholding Villiers these new referees adhered to De la Forest's initial and questionable critique; it is hard to see how Corro could have expected another outcome, or even why he bothered at all to discuss the *Tableau* further among his avowed enemies. Corro told his interlocutors that he had relied on the Zwinglian leader, Bullinger's 1566 articles of faith on predestination, free will, etc. for guidlines in composing the *Tableau*, and it is interesting that he quotes a passage from the work of a Danish follower of Melanchthon, Hemmingius, with approval. Cousin, on whose less than objective account of this proceeding we must rely, wrote sneeringly that despite the panel's vindication of the anti-*Tableau* forces " Corro is absolved by the silence of the bishops." [70]

Corro's letter to the Earl of Huntingdon, one of his English aristocratic benefactors, on January 18, 1571 disclosed his weary bitterness at his situation which seemed to consist of one futile altercation after another.[71] In it he noted, at last, his cognizance of Beza's relentless hostility: " While professing to admonish me in a friendly way, he affronts the whole Spanish nation... Neither can Beza by his letters render me heretic, nor can I... make him, the Frenchman, a friend of Spaniards." Corro blasted the French here for their " sophistical " and " hostile " conduct of the recent examination of the *Tableau*, and further renewed his description of them as " inquisitors." He observed that he had sent copies of that tract to Anglican bishops and German (?)

scholars, without adverse repercussions, and proudly noted that the 1570 editions had appeared with Archbishop Parker's permission. We also learn from this letter that among Corro's intimate " advisers " during his course of action was the Vidâme de Chartres, an eminent Huguenot lay leader then sojourning in England; [72] obviously Corro had not lost touch with his French connections, although it is curious that he did not apparently resume his relationship with the Cardinal de Châtillon, resident in the country until his death that year. We don't know if by now Corro had received Beza's " open " letter, previously mentioned. The quote Corro attributed to Beza was accompanied by an expression of uncertainty as to Beza's authorship. Two years later the first edition of Beza's correspondence appeared in which references to Corro were disguised with a single letter pseudonym; the 1575 second edition spelled out the Spaniard's name, however.[73] Corro's partial knowledge of Beza's antagonism sufficed in this instance, and " the solidarity [sic!] between Geneva and Corro could no longer be maintained." [74] In the Huntingdon letter Corro also acutely observed that " it was iniquitous that the accusers should also be the judges."

Among recent promotions in the Anglican hierarchy was that of Parker's chaplain, Richard Curteis, to the see of Chichester; in March of 1571 he was named by Sandys of London to chair still another commission to study, and presumably wind up the Corro affair. Given everything we have seen about men like Sandys, Parker, and Curteis in our context it is indisputable that with Grindal removed from the immediate scene Corro's well-placed friends now felt free to act more openly on his behalf, as the appointment of the superficially neutral Curteis suggests. On request the new commission received a resumé from the French and the Italians of their views, and while these were being considered the National Synod at La Rochelle advised the Anglican Church to keep a close watch on Corro and his writings.[75] Nothing indicates the Curteis group gave heed to this and similar warnings from France, nor that it even welcomed such admonitions from abroad concerning a matter technically belonging to Anglican jurisdiction alone. This commission, in fact, was destined to deliberate to no apparent end or purpose while Corro soon moved along a very different path. It seems to have been instituted solely for appearance's sake. Meanwhile, on July 3, 1571 Corro, apparently not in any specific response, wrote a long letter to Cousin defending anew the *Tableau* and the Théobon letter.[76] While reiterating the right to examine their work, Corro denounced the opinions of Arius, Pelagius, Osiander, Schwenkfeld, Servetus, the Anabaptists, and Rome. He also commented that if requested by "public authority" he would alter those obscurely-put passages in the *Tableau* which had bred misconceptions about his doctrines. There is little doubt that he had read every theologian he had repudiated to Cousin, and certainly was more than familiar with Catholic writings from his monastic days. From the start of his difficulties in London he had maintained that to read or ask about someone was not to subscribe to his views, and now he reiterated that consistent stand directly to his chief antagonist for the last time. Cousin thought otherwise, as did most of their compatriots. As McFadden suggested, this statement was probably drawn up at the request of Bishops Sandys and Curteis, prepatory to Corro's assumption of a new role, shortly to be discussed. On the other hand it is inconceivable that even the most moderate Anglican divine, however susceptible to secular influence in the powerful personages of Cecil and Leicester, would have allowed a man Corro's forthcoming post if he truly were a Servetian, Schwenkfelder, or what have you. Cousin lamented that circumstances surrounding this letter " shows... the reliance people had on [Corro]," [77] and this could refer only to his English supporters of high station in both church and state. The Frenchman probably never grasped how it came about that such otherwise worthy persons obstinately ignored the " proofs " of the Spaniard's doctrinal waywardness, nor could it have struck him and his supporters in London and elsewhere that their own assumptions regarding Corro might require serious review in consideration of that consistently sympathetic attitude towards him in these upper echelons of Elizabethan society.

Shortly after this Corro was elected Reader in Divinity by the benchers of the Inner and Middle Temples of the famous Inns

of Court, at the handsome yearly stipend of twenty pounds.[78]
In the years just preceding Corro's appointment the Inns had
been troubled by a considerable surge in recusancy, which
occasionally flared up thereafter.[79] It is fairly clear that he was
called in to combat this tendency, and that Sandys and Leicester,
the latter especially, set up Corro's "election" with the benchers.[80]
His preachings on *Romans* bore fruit when in 1574 he published
the *Dialogus Theologicus*, based on these lectures. The 1575
English edition is notable for its warm dedication to the Earl
of Leicester, from which we learn that almost from his arrival
in England the Earl had patronized Corro.[81] Leicester is also
credited here with having defended Corro against the personal
and doctrinal charges, after having listened to both sides like
a " great Alexander." [82] He hoped, too, that Leicester would
look favorably on this work " set out by me as a Confession
of... Faith to be examined and judged by the whole Church
of England." [83] With this statement we can assume Corro had
now broken formally with Calvinism, and was about to join
Anglicanism as a communicant; what better sponsor could one
find than the great Earl, the Queen's favorite? Archbishop
Parker described Corro's new work as showing his " purity of
doctrine... and his abomination of the troublesome sectaries." [84]
The *Dialogus Theologicus* is a sophisticated, if verbose effort to
balance grace, salvation by faith, and human action, and among
other things contained a strictly orthodox statement on the
Trinity. A copy of the work was also sent to Henry Bullinger
at Zurich by Corro for appraisal, but there is no record of an
answer.[85] The Spaniard had frequently claimed to be following
in Bullinger's theological footsteps, as we have seen.

The " sectaries " mentioned by Parker were the Puritans of
Corro's audience at the Inns. Richard Alvey, Master of the
Temple and thereby head of the clergy attached to the Inns,
inclined towards them, and in Parker's letter of March 14, 1574
to Grindal he noted that Alvey had appealed to him for advice
on how to handle Corro " whom his auditory doth mislike for
affirming free will, and his speaking not wisely on predestination,
and suspiciously uttering his judgment of Arianism, for which I

hear some... [will] forsake him." [86]   Later Parker observed that
" some took [his] part.   And it seems to have been the Discipli-
narians [i.e., Puritans] that were chiefly his adversaries." [87]   The
" his ", of course, was Corro.   Another contemporary, and
hostile view of his lectures at the Inns was William Barlow's.   He
frequented the Inns irregularly, but picked up a good deal of
gossip about the Spaniard as well as apparently attending some
of his preachings.   On January 21, 1575 he wrote to his friend
Josiah Simler in Zurich that Corro was " learned and eloquent,
but some worthy men entertain great doubts whether in respect
of piety he is to be compared with Villiers... he is a great admirer
of Castellion, of whose version of the Bible he declares... he
is a very bad [translator]... but if you speak about a paraphrase,
then says he, Castellion excels all... I was present at an excellent
lecture of his, in which he inveighed against the men of our age,
some of whom wish to be called Lutherans, others Calvinists,
etc., though neither Calvin nor Luther died for us; but we are
saved... by the blood of the Lamb slain for the sins of the
world... I wish he had stayed at Campostella." [88]   Corro was
expressing the notions he had published in his first work, the
Letter to the Lutheran Ministers...; the intervening years had
strengthened those earlier views.   The *Dialogus Theologicus*
carried forward the subtle watering down of predestination
begun in the *Tableau* as Corro moved nearer Anglicanism.   Not
surprisingly he attracted the fire of the Puritans, and given his
old connections in England, not to mention his bitterness towards
the Calvinists whom the Puritans frequently resembled and
imitated as far as possible, his joining the " Elizabethan " wing
of Anglicanism issued from the confluence of these factors.

The appearance in 1575 of the second edition of Beza's correspondence which firmly identified Corro to the Protestant world
as a malcontent has already been noted. Corro took it poorly
and appealed for advice in this regard to the eminent Sir Thomas
Smith. In his note to Smith he went into the history of the
entire affair and enclosed some pertinent documents. Smith
gave Corro's request careful and courteous attention, and his
reply revealed his acute comprehension of the matter when he

commented that both men had indulged too much in personal conflicts and had failed to search objectively for the truth.[89] For the rest Smith summarized the bones of contention involved, and observed in passing that both parties had some justice in their complaints of one another. However, he ignored any theological issue, advised both to calm down, and counseled Corro to write Beza in a " spirit of Christian charity," pointing out the harm his letters had done Corro and the Church. There is no evidence Corro put this suggestion into effect, and had he we cannot think Beza would have replied in a similar vein by this stage. Thus the 1575 edition of this correspondence marked Corro forever as an enemy of orthodox Calvinism, his own views and acts notwithstanding, not to add those of some of his supporters. One is reminded again of Hessels's dry analysis of these Beza-Corro exchanges: " but from none... does it appear what the disputes had really been about..."[90] Its appearance on the eve of Corro's highly controversial and bitterly contested attempt to obtain an Oxford degree ensured the ensuing furor, shortly to be explored; the Puritan divines of that university had as great a respect for Beza's opinions as had the Consistories of the Strangers' Churches.

3. FROM THE INNS TO OXFORD (1576 - 1579)

Probably this publication decided Corro and his supporters to reach for something at once concrete and universally respected so as to negate in some way the force of Beza's damning letters. Cecil, now Lord Burghley, was Chancellor of Cambridge University while the Earl of Leicester held that same post at Oxford. As Corro's application showed the recent statutes on dispensations for higher degrees were so severe at Cambridge that even Burghley's well-demonstrated favor could not prevail against them on his behalf.[91] Regulations were less restrictive at Oxford, however, and on March 5, 1576 Leicester himself wrote from court to recommend Corro to Vice-Chancellor Laurence Humphrey and Convocation.[92]   Specifically he asked that Corro be allowed to receive a doctorate in divinity with the usual minor degrees being waived, and he also petitioned for dispensing with the normal fees associated with the process in view of the applicant's " small " wealth.   In passing the Earl commented that " I doubt not but you will approve " Corro's credentials, and suggested that the more Humphrey and his peers became familiar with him the more they would realize he was indeed " fit for the degree."   On March 20 Corro followed up his patron's generous request with a lengthy plea of his own.[93]   Among other things he pointed out that the granting of so esteemed a doctorate in divinity in England would symbolize his purity of faith with respect to the Anglican Church, and also would please his fellow exiles and Spaniards everywhere.   He then described the above-mentioned failure at Cambridge, noting in passing the remote possibility of a mandated degree.   That Corro could fleetingly touch upon the kind of degree awarded by royal fiat indicates his optimism based clearly on the range of his intimate connections.   He concluded this appeal with the observation that this degree would confound his enemies and calumniators for once and for all, and he added here a derogatory reference to the puritanically-minded of the then ongoing vestiarian conflict. There can be no doubt that throughout his letter Corro was indirectly slashing out at the London Strangers' Churches. Whether Humphrey realized this from the first is debatable, but given his own Puritan tendencies Corro's gratuitous remark on the vestiarian affair was a blunder which must have aroused the Vice-Chancellor's ire and suspicions.   But a " request " from Leicester could not be ignored, or treated lightly.

On April 2 the Chancellor's recommendation and Corro's letter were read to Convocation.[94]   The latter voted the necessary waivers if Corro purged himself of dubious opinions by July next.   To some extent Corro's broad allusions to the necessity for his vindication through the degree undermined him and his supporters, and of course made clear his own over-confidence. The antiquarian chronicler of Oxford, Anthony à Wood, put the situation well: " ... it also being the intention of the Queen's

Council and high Commissioners of planting [Corro] among us, you cannot imagine what fears and jealousies were raised [among] the old Puritanical Doctors... fully bent to root out the dregs of Popery in the University, lest that which they labored in be frustrated by a stranger." [95] Since it must have been well known that Corro had been brought to the Inns of Court precisely to " root out the dregs of Popery " the raising of this false issue was clearly designed to screen the fact that Corro's application was merely another nexus for the continuing battle between the Puritan and moderate elements at Oxford. Furthermore there was collusion between the Oxford " Puritanical Doctors " and Corro's ancient antagonists from among the refugee Calvinists in London, which in a sense violated the unwritten code which had kept the native Puritans and " visiting " Calvinists apart. [96]

On April 20 Corro's old and formidable judge and opponent, Pierre Loiseleur de Villiers, applied for the doctorate in divinity, requesting the same special conditions Corro had. [97] His plea was granted immediately, almost in spite of Villiers's belated hesitations. [98] At approximately this time the French, Italian, and Dutch Strangers' Churches of London prepared a joint statement excorciating Corro through his writings, lectures, and conversations. From this *Theses and Antitheses*, [99] copies of which were sent to Oxford, the Archbishop of Canterbury, now Edmund Grindal, and the Bishop of London, it is quite clear that the London Calvinists had kept close watch on Corro since his break with them in 1571. In case the new document was unclear a covering letter of explanation was enclosed with the copies. Its timing was perfectly designed to inflame the situation at Oxford. Sandys, of course, doubtless remained unmoved, while Grindal had his hands full in his conflict with the Queen over prophesying.

On June 7 John Reynolds of Corpus Christi, one of the militant Puritans at the University (who had a brother recently gone over to Catholicism !), wrote Humphrey protesting against any proposed concession to Corro. [100] He summarized the Spaniard's controversial past, stressing Beza's implacable hostility to him. Reynolds suggested that Leicester really intended to give his protégé a permanent readership once the doctorate was obtained, as he had at the Inns, which would "raise such flames in our University" which "the Lord doth know, whether ever they shall be quenched." He notes that Corro had recently tutored the highly heterodox Francesco Pucci, recently expelled from Oxford by Humphrey himself.[101] He dismissed the supporters Corro had in high places, calling their letters on his behalf evidence they had been "partly... misinformed by others, partly deceived by his own fair promises." Reynolds ended with an impassioned appeal to Humphrey "that nothing be done in the time of your government, whereby the Papist may be strengthened, the faithful discomforted, the glory of God hindered, the power of Satan advanced." To what possible extent this represented Reynolds's attempt to compensate for his brother's desertion of "the faithful" is unknown,[102] but it probably accounts for the quasi-hysteria characterizing his letter. It was hardly a realistic appraisal of matters.

Six days afterwards Convocation decided that Corro could not take the degree unless statements from Grindal and Sandys could be produced testifying to his orthodoxy since his arrival in England, and it further requested he purge himself before Humphred and the Oxford theologians.[103] This pronouncement followed the consideration of more letters from Corro and his supporters and an examination of the *Theses and Antitheses*. Not only had the conditional victory of April 2 been nullified, but the Earl of Leicester, and in a sense through him the government, had been severely rebuffed. All concerned must have known that Grindal would never certify Corro as doctrinally safe by this time, and Sandys, of course, would not suffice alone. Leicester, however, while obviously not wishing to go against the majority of his university was not the man to take so blatant a rejection of his influence without any response; on June 23 Humphrey was relieved of the Vice-Chancellorship and replaced by a more tractable person.[104]

Leicester's role in all this requires some extended comment. Traditionally he is frequently associated, rather loosely, with the Puritan faction in the governing classes, although implicitly there is a political rather than religious emphasis here. In fact Villliers was a more likely candidate for the Earl's support than Corro, given their comparative backgrounds. Considering Leicester's disastrous career in the Netherlands in 1586-7 and Villiers's influential role against him then this academic flurry in 1576 may have had belated repercussions. However, without going further afield, the observation of a recent historian that Leicester stood " for the established church reformed, purified, but Anglican..." suggests accurately why he could not support the styles of religion increasingly demanded by the Puritan groups, however much he may have sympathized with them in many matters.[105] Probably more important here was his history as a patron of Italian Protestant refugees in England; Corro after all was a member of that church for a time. While many of the latter people may have been drawn to the Earl because of his reputation as the protector of Puritans,[106] it is interesting that one of his more famous such proteges was Giacomo Concio (Acontius), whose denunciations of capital punishment for heretics and friendship with persons like Reina and Corro placed him well beyond the pale of orthodox Calvinism; his talents as a fortifications engineer, however, earned him the Queen's protection and a handsome pension, as well as Leicester's not inconsiderable patronage.[107] Despite some differences the attitudes of men like Concio resembled those of Castellio regarding the treatment of heresy, and so broadly approached Corro's own views as described. If we can safely assume that Leicester considered religious harmony as the basis for political unity and strength, and followed his royal mistress in her pragmatic approach concerning the individual conscience and related matters, then his consistent support of men like Concio and Corro against the fulminations of Puritans and refugee Calvinists alike becomes understandable. As a monarchist and English-style politique Leicester would have encountered no difficulty in repudiating Puritan demands for a Geneva type of church discipline and government, publicly assisting a Corro and yet acting as the champion of Puritanism in other areas. Perhaps we need a firmer definition of this " Puritanism ", not

63

to mention a study of Leicester on the scale of Read's volumes on Walsingham and Cecil. Of course, we must keep in mind that to him the Corro affair was pretty far down his list of matters of state; still, it affords a fresh angle of approach to the man and related problems.

Although he was still formally attached to the Inner and Middle Temples there is some indication that at least as soon as the latter part of 1577 Corro either was working for or had already obtained a lectureship at Oxford.[108]   While we know very little about him from the summer of 1576, following the destruction of his hopes for a degree, to the summer of 1578 by which time he had definitely gained the more limited objective of the lecturing position at Oxfrod, this period saw a spate of reeditions of some of his works in English. These seemed clearly timed to ensure success at the university, for in the granting of this position Convocation said it had been satisfied by Corro's thorough exposition of his views in recent public appearances, and it follows logically that the Oxonians had also familiarized themselves with his writings, so recently renewed for their un doubted edification.[109] Circumstances, too, had improved Corro's prospects. Grindal, in the midst of his prophesying conflict with the Queen, was in no position to interfere. Sandy's successor in London, John Aylmer, proved a very forward advocate for the Spaniard, while the Oxonians must have recalled Humphrey's dismissal following their rejection of Corro's appeal for the doctorate as they mulled over his application for a lectureship.

From the sparse evidence it is plausible to think Corro was shuttling back and forth between Oxford and London during the second half of 1577, and Convocation's citing his recent edifying public statements of his beliefs probably referred to these occasional appearances on the campus. An unhappy by-product, however, was Corro's growing neglect of his obligations to the benchers at the Inns. After prolonged discussion, which included Corro's attempt to get a testimonial from the two Temples to further his cause at Oxford, he was dropped from the Readerships.[110] There is no doubt that in the perfunctory manner he fulfilled his duties there during his last months Corro acted in a depressing style. Clearly he no longer cared seriously about matters there, confident as he was of the successful outcome of his new application to Oxford,[111] but this hardly excuses his conduct towards the institutions which had so well supported him in the past seven years.[112] Indeed at this time he resembles nothing so much as a latter-day member of the academic market-place.

On July 7, 1578 Convocation first took formal note of Corro's new request, which was supported by Leicester and the Royal Commissioners who had recently put him through his theological paces.[113] The Strangers' Churches of London sent in letters of denunciation. Corro appeared to proclaim his desire to clear himself, and Convocation organized a committee from its ranks to assist in that purpose. Among its members was Laurence Humphrey, now President of Magdalen College, and John Reynolds. On July II Corro declared his beliefs before Convocation, indicated his wish to reside at Oxford for the next several months in order to satisfy everyone concerning his doctrines, and promised to abide by the judgment of the Royal Commissioners or the majority of the University's doctors.[114] The former's verdict was certain to be favorable in view of its backing of Corro already noticed, and it is curious that he did not talk about Convocation's committee in this context.[115] For the ensuing twelve weeks of the Michaelmas term he lectured in theology at Christ Church College, taking over that post from Humphrey, which must have given Corro an ironical bit of satisfaction.[116] Early in 1579 were added to this position, formally called *Censor Theologicus*, a similar lectureship in divinity at Merton Hall and catechist for St. Mary's, Gloucester, and Hert Halls.[117] Hart and Gloucester had fairly well-grounded reputations for Catholicism. When we recall that in his initial dealings with Oxford there had been some imputation that granting Corro the degree would be a step towards the old faith his appointments as catechist to these halls forcibly underlines the flimsiness of those oblique slanders and reminds us that Corro's supporters rightly considered his forensic talents as a useful weapon against recusancy. It is appropriate to note here that during the negociations leading to his Oxford positions the Calvinists accused him of " diverse crimes and heresies... believed by... especially the zealous and Puritanical party " at the University and Corro " being suspected [hitherto] of heresy, now was accused of Popery". Furthermore the " Bishop of Chester [rose to] deplore and lament the preaching and publishing of Popish errors among us The doctrine [of pure Protestantism] began first to be notably corrupted... by Corro... and his writings... notoriously known to have been full of many erroneous and fantastical opinions."[118] Corro's enemies were trotting out rather desperately the old, contradictory charges which only the most closed-minded at Oxford could reconcile and accept. No doubt the more favorable atmosphere there, the more tactful handling of matters by Corro himself, as well as his supporters, and his recent expositions of his ideas in print and in assembly, as it were, made it much easier for even some who had turned him away in 1576 to accept him just two years later. And certainly few could swallow wholly again the notion that any man could simultaneously adhere to Rome, Servetus, and Schwenkfeld.

4. Last Years: The Prebends and Final Controversies (1579 - 1591)

On May 16, 1579 Corro published his *Paraphrase and Commentary on Ecclesiastes*, and in the dedicatory preface to Sir Thomas Bromley he wrote: " The best reformation would be the renascence by which Christians would set aside their differences."[119] Corro's own life lent a powerful undercurrent beneath this baldy irenic plea, whose fulfillment was as far off as ever. Ten days later he took out denization papers.[120] He was now an Englishman as well as an Anglican, and on November 22, 1579 Corro wrote Leicester's secretary, Arthur Atey, asking him to remind the Earl gently of his promise to consider him for a bishopric.[121] In this letter he also alluded to a testimonial given him by the Oxford doctors to aid his new career, but this document is not extant. It must have symbolized the supreme vindication at the University for Corro. During the winter of 1579-80 he spent almost all his time pursuing ecclesiastical preferment, to such an extent that Dean Matthew, one of his consistent supporters at Oxford, had to write Atey, asking him to "persuade Corro to repair to Oxford as soon... as he could."[122] The Spaniard's lax notions about the execution of his momentary obligations remained even now one of his consistent weaknesses. From the same letter it becomes clear that Leicester was thinking about getting Corro an advowson at Christ Church as well as a prebend, but Matthew, now Vice-Chancellor, observed that with the approaching end of his own tenure Corro might run into troubles at the University. The latter returned to Oxford shortly thereafter, and Matthew's misgivings proved premature.[123]

It took perhaps a bit longer than Corro and his patrons had anticipated, but finally on March 29, 1582 Bishop Aylmer installed him in St. Paul's as prebend of Harleston.[124] In the interim he continued at his Oxford posts, and added a second prebend three years later.[125] But his difficulties remained still to be fully allayed.

The French refugee, Peter Baro (n), was at Cambridge and like Corro, a protegé of Lord Burghley. During 1579-80 the two exiles had "talked shop" at Baro's lodgings. The latter's publications had also aroused the wrath of orthodox Calvinism, and frequently he was bracketed with Corro unfavorably. On September 14, 1580 Baro wrote De Laune, Cousin's successor, defending himself against the combined assaults of Calvinists and English Puritans such as Laurence Chadderton, Corró's successor at the Inns, and the famous Walter Travers.[126] Baro conceded that he had had conversations with Corro, but insisted that they did not agree on all particulars. He denied being a member of the notorious Family of Love, and was certain Corro was not either. Not without bitterness Baro observed that he was accused of denying reprobation by Travers, who was shortly to attack Corro as well, merely "because he had heard I had spoken with Corro," and he suggested that given the hatred of Corro current in these circles if it were rumored the Spaniard denied the Lord then it would be assumed Baro had said the same.

Baro eventually resigned from Cambridge, only to turn up at Oxford where his views created a substantial stir during 1595-6, four years after Corro's death.[127] It seems reasonable to deduce that despite their lack of absolute agreement on everything Baro was influenced by Corro, if for no other reason than having common enemies and patrons, and the latter of course tended to support irenicist-politique types as we have seen. In his astute study of Oxford and Cambridge in this period Mark Curtis sees Baro as a contributor towards early English Arminianism and part of the native reaction against orthodox Calvinist views on election.[128] Corro, on the other hand, is presented by Curtis as an isolated, if similar phenomenon, lacking Baro's greater impact. But Baro's letter to De Laune establishes a direct link between the two. More broadly, Corro's years of lecturing and writing at the Inns and Oxford, as well as his strong and conti-nuing support from high places in England suggest at least that he was a minor and unisolated phenomenon. There seems to be some truth in the notion that he, too, was a precursor of Arminia-nism, and it is striking that in 1618 the Dutch Remonstrant, Doede van Amsweer, brought out new editions of several of Corro's works.[129] At any rate the new outlook spreading among certain Anglican circles from the 1590's, characterized by an emphasis on God's grace as a free gift to all men in Christ, does not seem far removed from Corro's strictures, and given his career from 1571 as outlined there is scant reason to discount his influence.

Corro cemented his ties of patronage by becoming the confidant of the Prior of Crato, pretender to the Portuguese throne, during his stay in England; he alternately spied on Don Antonio for his adopted country and tried to convert him to Protestantism.[130] Corro also moved in increasingly exalted circles. Among his new acquaintances during the 1580's were Sir Philip Sidney, the diplomat Sir Amias Paulet, whose sons he tutored, and Jean Hotman.[131] The latter was the son of François, the famous jurist of Bourges, who in 1567 had been among those consulted by the London French in preparing their case against Corro.[132] During his stay in England the younger Hotman was patronized by the Leicester clique, and his once-orthodox Calvinism gave way to a profound irenicism, which was to inform his work later under Henry IV.[133] For Corro the wheel in this regard had turned full circle very satisfactorily indeed.

One last battle remained. On March 3, 1582, while the first prebend was still pending, Leicester's agent in the Low Countries, William Herle, sent his master a lengthy description of his interview with Francesco Pucci, once Corro's student.[134] In a very confused manner Pucci had attacked Corro, calling him one of the most " dangerous " persons around, and suggested he was a complete hypocrite religiously. As Herle commented, however, Pucci " also had strange conceits of religion." In fact, the Italian had moved from Catholicism to Calvinism to a debate in Basel with Fausto Sozzini which caused his expulsion even from that hospitable city of Erasmus, and eventually to martyrdom in Rome in 1597. As Luigi Firpo has shown Pucci ended up rejected by and rejecting all the organized faiths of the day. What motivated him to try to undermine Corro is unknown. While Herle's report clearly failed to deny Corro his prebent it is possible its contents somehow were communicated to his traditional opponents in London. Leicester himself intervened. On May 7, 1582, having heard that " certain rumors " at Oxford reported Corro had been " detained prisoner " in London, he sent the Spaniard back to the University with letters for the current Vice-Chancellor, Oliver Withington.[135] He ordered a resolution of the entire business for the sake of this " poor man," and set aside May 17 to hear arguments in person from Corro and his foes; Leicester specifically singled out the London French for representation. A week later Withington gathered his materials and shipped them to his Chancellor. He had, he wrote, " caused your letters to be read openly in the Convocation house " on May 13 and no one had come forward to accuse Corro for his doctrines or his morals.[136] Unfortunately no record remains of the May 17 confrontation. Armed with the Oxford document and entering a " court " presided over by his warmest patron Corro had nothing to fear, and doubtless enjoyed his ancient antagonists' discomfiture. Thereafter no such troubles arose, and he continued peacefully at Oxford and his prebends. On August 26, 1584 the new minister of the London French, Jean Castrol, wrote Beza gloomily that " we are not yet persecuted; we only learn that our open adversaries, for instance Corro, are in credit with the Queen... We are told Her Majesty has entertained great suspicion and displeasure against us from the false reports." [137] Whether or not Corro was one of those spreading these " false reports " about the Strangers' Churches is not clear from Castol's bitter remarks, but probably he could not resist any opportunity coming his way to discredit the refugee Calvinists of the capital who had so often acted underhandedly against him period. Certainly the collusion between them and the Puritans in cases like his and Baro's must have been known to the government; " false reports " or not that would have sufficed easily to anger Elizabeth, who took a traditionally dim view of such rapport.

One controversy involved Corro indirectly, and is worth a brief notice. In March, 1585, Richard Alvey, the Puritan Master of the Temple at the Inns died, and the subsequently famous Richard Hooker succeeded him. Walter Travers, then a Reader at the Inns, attacked the appointment, commenting that Hooker was weak on predestination " not unlike that wherewith Corro sometime troubled this church." [138] Travers was continuing his recent assaults upon Corro and Baro as well as Alvey's traditions at the Temple, but his opposition broke against Bishop Aylmer's staunch recommendation of Hooker. Aylmer, it is appropriate to repeat, had installed Corro at Harleston.

For reasons totally unknown Corro apparently lost or, more likely resigned his Oxford positions during 1586, although he chose to remain in residence with his family nearby instead of living at one his prebends. [139] While Leicester had just departed for a disastrous tour of duty in the Netherlands he had appointed another of Corro's friends, Thomas Bromley, as deputy Chancellor; this rules out the possibility of a fall from favor as far as all available evidence indicates. Although we hear nothing of it perhaps failing health dictated this retirement; by June 13, 1589 Corro was writing Jean Hotman about his weakening eyesight. [140] For the remainder of his days Corro, helped by various persons such as John Thorie, worked on new editions of his works, brought out the *Spanish Grammar* and edited a version of Alonso Valdés's *Dialogo de las cosas acacidas en Roma*.[141] On March 30, 1591 he passed away in London.[142]

---

[1] Schickler, I: pp. 167-78, 3: pp. 73-86; *BW* 3: pp. 91-98, 100-03.

[2] See note 5 ch. 1 above.

[3] Hessels 3 i: pp. 45-46. On Farías see *HSP* 38 (London, 1937): pp. 59-60, 63, 69-70, 103-04 and Luigi Firpo, " La Chiesa italiana di Londra nel Cinquecento e i suoi rapporti con Ginebra ", in *Ginevra e L'Italia* (Florence, 1959): pp. 364 ff most recently; on Sánchez see *HSP* 10 i: pp. 391, 448; 10 ii: pp. 202, 323, 428 (London, 1900-08); *Werken der Marnix-Vereeniging* Ser. I, 1 (Utrecht, 1870): pp. 266-67.

[4] E.g. Hessels 3 i: pp. 48, 50; *BW* 3: pp. 10-11, 29-31. Cousin, however, paid tribute to Corro's renown as a preacher even here.

[5] *BW* 3: p. 29.

[6] These Montargis and Antwerp statements are no longer extant, unfortunately. See Hessels 3 i: pp. 17, 47-49 for relevant data. Regarding the former testimonial the London French complained that Corro " does not seem to resemble the great praises given him " from there, *ibid*. 3 i: p. 49.

[7] The Des Gallars letter is no longer extant; for the others see *ibid*., 3 i: pp. 48-49 and Böhmer, " Corro ", pp. 203-04.

[8] Technically all refugee churches in the capital's vicinity were under the Bishop of London's jurisdiction and supervision. Given Corro's close relations with influential persons such as the Earl of Leicester and William Cecil from this time on our suggestion seems pausible all the more. This first commission was apparently entirely Anglican. For some still valuable elucidation of Grindal's position and outlook in cases like these see John Strype, *Annals of the Reformation* (Oxford, 1824) 1: p. 174.

[9] *PSP* 19 (Cambridge, 1848): pp. 313-14; Schickler 3: pp. 73-74; Böhmer, " Corro," pp. 208 f.

[10] Hessels 3 i: pp. 48-50. Ironically one of Hotman's sons later was to be associated with, and apparently influenced by Corro; see notes 131-133 below.

[11] Hessels 3 i: p. 50.

[12] *Ibid*. 2: pp. 271-75; *BW* 3: pp. 31 ff; J. Strype, *History of the Life and Acts of Edmund Grindal* (London, 1710): pp. 159-60.

[13] Same as first citation in note 12 above.

[24] Böhmer, " Corro," pp. 206-07.

[15] Hessels 3 i: pp. 52-55.

[16] It is most likely that it was through Marcus Pérez during his stay in Antwerp that Corro first was brought favorably to the notice of persons like Cecil. For Pérez's correspondence and occasional direct contact with Gresham, et al see the article ¦cited in note 27 Pt. I ch. ii above.

[17] *PSP* 33 (Cambridge, 1853) pp. 339-40.   See also the dedication to Leicester by Corro in the 1575 *Theological Dialogue*, discussed below, which sharply points to a very early connection with him.

[18] The French, at this time, maintained a dim view of the Italian Church as a refuge for various dubious persons. E.g. Hessels 3 i: p. 54; Strype, *Annals* 2 i: p. 41.

[19] Strype, *Annals* 4: p. 571; Roland Bainton, *Travail of Religious Liberty* (NY, 1958 paper ed.): p. 162; *HSP* 10 i: p. 403. The Duchess was the very Protestant daughter of a Spanish lady-in-waiting to Catherine of Aragon, and a prominent benefactress of religious refugees.

[20] Hessels 3 i: pp. 58-59.

[21] A copy is in the Bibliothèque publique et universitaire de Genève, Ms. fr. 407, Correspondance ecclésiastique, 7: 28 recto to verso (from McFadden p. 317 n 3); it is reprinted in Böhmer, " Corro," pp. 208-09. It seems that Corro obtained a copy of the Théobon note from Grindal, and that the latter initially warmly supported him; furthermore, given Corro's penury at this time it is clear someone financed the printing of the " Apology."   Considering Grindal's subsequent attitude towards Corro, which seems to commence with the " Apology's" appearance some concrete disentangling of his motives and views are in order. We suggest some below; McFadden does not seem quite aware of the apparent direct contradiction in Grindal's attitude towards Corro before and after the " Apology "; see pp. 317 ff.

[22] Schickler 3: pp. 74-77 reprints the letter; we paraphrase from it.

[23] See note 21 above and Hessels 3 i: p. 60.

[24] *Ibid.* 3 i: pp. 81-82.

[25] *Ibid.* 3 i: pp. 58-59.

[26] *Ibid.* 3 i: p. 60. In this note the French claimed Grindal had told them in advance that Corro's letter was full of " gall and venom."

[27] Reprinted in Böhmer, " Corro," pp. 209-14, it is the sole one extant from seven Corro sent Beza during the autumn and winter of 1567-68. For further discussion of it see *GN* 3: p. 178. Corro attacked Morel in it, which apparently added to Beza's growing dislike of the Spaniard,

and the latter's effort to recall his student days at Lausanne under Beza, et al fell equally flat.

28 Hessels 3 i: pp. 62-72 has the full text; see also *BW* 3: p. 117. We have retained the original French title, of course.

29 Of course such evidence well might merely have failed to survive the centuries. In his July 15, 1568 letter to Grindal already cited Corro defended himself against the London French Church's jurisdiction by appealing to the National Synods and his Antwerp Church. The latter, of course, was driven underground or dispersed since March, 1566 while the former had already condemned him at Vertueil in September, 1567. Corro's approach suggests a kind of inept subterfuge which Grindal may have seen through and which accounts further for his increasing coolness towards Corro. Clearly neither side, or all three in fact if one sees Grindal as the third, was above double-dealing at several levels and instances. In a sense one can sympathize with Grindal, caught between the likes of Cousin and Corro.

30 Hessels 3 i: pp. 34, 67. Even McFadden, who tends to sympathize with the French is uneasy in his discussion of this. See pp. 198 ff; cf. *BW* 3: p. 40.

31 Hessels 3 i: pp. 70-71.

32 *Ibid*. 3 i: pp. 63-64; Schickler 3: p. 84-85.

33 Schickler 3: pp. 84-85; *BW* 3: pp. 89-91.

34 Same as note 33 above and *GN* 3: p. 169.

35 *BW* 3: p. 39; Schickler 3: p. 84.

36 These letters are in the *Epist. Theol.* (1575): pp. 243-61. See *BW* 3: p. 41 and *GN* 3: pp. 169 ff for comment. A glance at E. H. Harbison, *Age of the Reformation* (Cornell U. Pr., 1955 paper ed.): pp. 6 f and G. Matthews, *News and Rumor in Renaissance Europe* (NY, 1959 paper ed.): p. 20 will show why Beza's letters could never have arrived in time to affect this decision, either way.

37 See note 78 Pt. I ch. ii above the McFadden's listing; a French version which we have consulted is found in *GN* 3: pp. 155-64 and in Hessels 3 i: pp. 75-80.

38 De la Forest's censures are in Paris, Bibliothèque Nationale, 43077 Ms Dupuy 103, 67 recto to 69 recto which follow a Latin version of the *Tableau* with marginal comments, 56 recto to 66 recto (from McFadden, pp. 355 n. 3, 356 n. 1 ff).

39 Quoted in Schickler 1: pp. 175-76 note. On this point, however, the observation of Böhmer in *BW* 3: p. 65 n. 123 is still pertinent: " That there is no mention of the eternal Trinity does not prove antitrinitarianism," made with reference to the (c. 1570) *Monas Theologica*, authorship uncertain, occasionally attributed to Corro. See McFadden's discussion of the work, pp. 383-84, ch. 37, and his belief Corro did

write it. However, as McFadden concedes, Corro never claimed it whereas his enemies in London insisted he composed it. It is a far clearer statement of a unitarian kind than Corro's other writings allow, and it is not surprising Corro's foes tried to convince all concerned he was its author.

[40] Hessels 2: p. 988.

[41] *BW* 3: pp. 41, 83-89.

[42] *Ibid.* 3: pp. 41-43, 83-89. All things considered it seems very likely he sent her there to provoke an incident.

[43] *Ibid.*, 3: p. 89.

[44] *PSP* 19: pp. 309-12.

[45] *Ibid.*, 19: p. 310.

[46] *Ibid.*, 19: pp. 309 n. 3, 310 n. 1, 311 n. 1.

[47] Hessels 2: p. 329; *BW* 3: p. 45. Grindal must have been getting fairly tired; in the course of this he told Cousin " I do not quite understand your phrases."

[48] *BW* 3: p. 96.

[49] *Ibid.*, 3: p. 93 and note 21 above, 112 verso. One of the Flemings was an elder of the Italian Church (from McFadden, p. 362 n. 2.)

[50] Same as note 49 above, 40 recto to 47 recto, 62 recto to 119 verso (from McFadden, p. 363 n. 2, 4).

[51] *BW* 3: pp. 93-96.

[52] E.g. *Ibid.* 3: pp. 92, 95.

[53] Jean Jacquot, " Sébastien Castellion et l'Angleterre," *Bibliothèque d'Humanisme et Renaissance* 15 (1953): p. 24.

[54] Same as note 52 above.

[55] *Ibid.*, 3: p. 92.

[56] *State Papers Foreign*. Gen. Series. Elizabeth (S.P. 70): 109 folio 8 (from McFadden p. 366 n. 1).

[57] See note 47 above.

[58] Hessels 3 i: pp. 95-97.

[59] *Ibid.*, 3 i: p. 45.

[60] *BW* 3: p. 56.

[61] *Ibid.*, 3: p. 49.

[62] *Ibid.*, 3: p. 96.

[63] *Ibid.*, 3: p. 41, n. 97.

[64] *Ibid.*, 3: p. 49 and *GN* 3: pp. 166-67.

[65] *BW* 3: pp. 48-49, 96.

74

[66] Same as note 65 above and *ibid*. 3: p. 97 Cf. *GN* 3: p. 166 for an unsympathetic view of Corro's actions here.

[67] Hessels 3 i: p. 135; *BW* 3: p. 56; *HSP* 10 ii: p. 21. The lengthy L. Firpo article on the London Italian Church cited in note 3 above is especially valuable for the years 1570-90 where he is able to rely on the " Verbali de Concistro della Chiesa italiana di Londra " which start in the former year. P. 364 ff reveal a tragic struggle revolving about the rivalry between Corro and one of his former companions at San Isidro, Cypriano de Valera, which violently split the Spanish adherents of this church. Francisco Farías, once both men's monastic prior, held out longest in favor of Corro even after the latter had left the congregation for all practical purposes, but he, too, was brought to admit to Corro's errors, etc. by the spring of 1572, long after the other supporters had dropped away in order to maintain their attachment to this church. Valera seems to have been jealous of Corro's leadership of the Spanish in the Italian Church, which for unknown reasons he had joined sometimes between 1568 and 1570 after first attending the French Church. He also seems to have played a role in the Italian Church similar to Balthazar Sánchez's in the French one concerning Corro, at least. Farías, too, had started out in the French congregation after the collapse of Reina's Spanish Church in 1564-65, but by 1582 he had rejoined it. The scanty data give no reason for these very odd church membership shifts; see *HSP* 10 i: pp. 260, 387-89, 462; ii: pp. 115, 294 on him.

[68] *PSP* 19: p. 312 n. 1.

[69] Hessels 3 i: pp. 108-23, 129-38; *BW* 3: pp. 50-56. It is curious that Corro's eagerness to reveal his sources somewhat confounded the Consistory; see *BW* 3: p. 54.

[70] *BW* 3: p. 55-56.

[71] Hessels 3 i: p. 180; *BW* 3: pp. 52-53. He was Leicester's brother-in-law, and in 1573 Villiers had dedicated a work to him; see Boer p. 54.

[72] *BW* 3: p. 53-55.

[73] In the 1573 edition Corro was referred to as " N "; in the 1575 edition by name, as noted. See McFadden's examples on pp. 412 n. 3, 436 n. 1.

[74] *GN* 3: p. 178.

[75] *BW* 3: pp. 57-58, 100-01. McFadden has a lengthy excerpt from the Synod's original statement on pp. 395-96 n. 3.

[76] Hessels 3 i: pp. 144-46; *BW* 3: pp. 58-60.

[77] *BW* 3: pp. 58-59.

[78] McFadden, ch. 26 goes exhaustively into this and related technical matters of the Inns. The Earl of Leicester lived in the fashionable

district near the Inns, and patronized many of its students and staff; see Rosenberg, pp. 135, 177-80 on this, and J. Strype, *Life and Acts of Matthew Parker* (Oxford, 1821) 2: pp. 402-03 which indicates very surprinsigly that Grindal had a hand in obtaining this post for Corro.

[79] Strype, *Parker* 2: pp. 73-75.

[80] This is made abundantly clear by Corro's remarks in the dedication to the *Theol. Dial.* cited in note 17 above. The University of Michigan library's microfilm copy is short-title catalog 5786, carton 953.

[81] " Dedicatory epistle," *Theol. Dial.*

[82] Same as note 81 above.

[83] Same as note 81 above.

[84] Strype, *Parker* 2: p. 403.

[85] McFadden, ch. 28, is very thorough on this. The relevant correspondence is in *BW* 3: pp. 103-04; Strype, *Parker* 2: p. 404; *PSP* 51: pp. 254-55. Sandys and Bullinger seem to have been steady correspondents during these years.

[86] *PSP* 33: p. 476.

[87] Strype, *Parker* 2: pp. 402-03.

[88] *PSP* 51: pp. 261-62; *BW* 3: 62-63 which suggests that even a careful, reliable scholar like Böhmer could be impressed by such fulminations.

[89] Bodleian Library. Ms. Top. Oxon e 5: pp. 69-70 (from McFadden, p. 436 n. 2).

[90] Hessels 2: p. 988.

[91] Corro's application to Cambridge, referred to here, is not extant. McFadden, pp. 450 ff analyzes and compares the relevant regulations at the two schools. See J. B. Mullinger, *The University of Cambridge* (Cambridge, 1884) 2: especially pp. 231-32 and Anthony à Wood, *History and Antiquities of the University of Oxford* (Oxford, 1794): 2 i: pp. 179 ff.

[92] Wood 2 i: p. 179. Leicester's letter is cited in full in McFadden, pp. 446-47 and n. 1 from Univ. Oxon. Arch. KK9 1564 1582: folio 207 verso.

[93] Cited in *Polem.* pp. 5-8.

[94] Wood 2 i: p. 180.

[95] Same as note 94 above.

[96] As recently as 1573 the Privy Council had told the refugee churches not to receive native Puritans, and they complied. See Strype, *Annals* 2 i: pp. 419-22. A strong indication of such " cooperation " was that Villiers was receiving reports of Convocation's discussions of himself and Corro from an anonymous Oxonian. See *Polem.*, pp. 11-12.

[97] Same archival citation as note 92 above.

[98] *Polem.*, pp. 14-15; cf. Boer, pp. 54 ff.

[99] Printed in *Polem.*, pp. 30-60.

[100] The text is in Wood 2 i: pp. 180-82.

[101] *GN* 3: pp. 179-80; *BW* 3: p. 68. More recently see L. Firpo, "Francesco Pucci in Inghilatera," *Revue internationale de Philosophie* 5 (1951): pp. 158-73. See also the same author's "Francesco Pucci a Basilea," *Mediaevo e Rinascimiento. Studi in honore di B. Nardi* (Florence, 1955): pp. 257-95. I am indebted to Mr. John Tedeschi of the Newberry Library, Chicago for these references.

[102] On this see John Bossy, "Elizabethan Catholicism," *Crisis in Europe* (NY, 1965): p. 231.

[103] Wood 2 i: p. 184; *BW* 3: pp. 68-69. McFadden produces the archival evidence, pp. 464-65 and notes.

[104] *BW* 3: p. 69. It must be added, however, that this office was annual and did not possess tenure.

[105] Joel Hurstfield, "Some Elizabethans," *History* 47 (February, 1962): p. 26.

[106] Rosenberg, p. 57. It is interesting that not only did Villiers lead the anti-Leicester faction in the Netherlands in 1585-86 but his theology, to the distress of many, took a very irenicist turn during the '80's, very like Corro's, in fact, although there is no evidence they were in touch in the later period. See Boer, pp. 107 ff; McFadden, pp. 549 ff; and the author's article cited in note 54, Pt. I ch. ii above.

[107] Rosenberg, pp. 54-55. She sees this as an instance of Leicester's "italianate" tendencies. Concio, and Reina, had defended the Dutch pastor, Hamstede, whose attack on capital punishment for Anabaptists in England early in the 1560's had angered the Queen and led directly to his excommunication from his church and eventual departure from the country.

[108] McFadden summarizes the unclear data on p. 474.

[109] Univ. Oxon. Arch. KK9: folio 260 recto (from McFadden, pp. 484-85 n. 1).

[110] McFadden summarizes details here, pp. 474 ff, using standard secondary accounts of the Inns with some archival materials.

[111] It is interesting to learn that at this time the London Calvinists still had an eye on Corro, which prefaced their interference in Oxford; e.g. Hessels 3 i: pp. 501-04.

[112] Nonetheless he did not lose at least several of the important friends he had made there, such as Sir Thomas Bromley and Sir Christopher Hatton; the former will come under discussion again, while the latter was the object of Corro's dedication in his 1587 *Dialogus in epistolam*

D. Pauli ad Romanos.

[113] Same as note 109 above.

[114] Same as note 113 above.

[115] Despite Humphrey and Reynolds's presence on it is appears to have been well " stacked " with Leicester's " creatures." The new annual Vice-Chancellor was one Martin Colepepper, which augured well for Corro as he represented, to McFadden anyway (p. 486) the very pinnacle of Leicester's intrusion into university affairs and power struggles.

[126] Wood 2 i: p. 195; Strype, *Parker* 2: p. 404; Mark Curtis, *Oxford and Cambridge in Transition, 1558-1642* (Oxford, 1959): p. 212. Toby Matthew, Dean of Christ Church, was another of Leicester's favorites at the university. For Corro's salaries see McFadden's figures, pp. 749 ff based on the Batell and Disbursement Books of Christ Church College.

[117] Same as note 116 above.

[118] Wood 2 i: pp. 196-97.

[119] *BW* 3: p. 71 n. 135. Böhmer has cited this remark in his text, and in this note compiles an array of Protestant and Catholic favorable views of the sentiment then and afterwards.

[120] *HSP* 8: pp. xl, 53. Bromley helped smooth Corro's way in this.

[121] Reprinted in *BW* 3: p. 105. Whether or not Corro actually meant a bishopric *per se* is unclear, for we do know Leicester at the time was working to get him a prebend or an advowson, and certainly nothing greater. See *CSP* Domestic 136 (1547-80): p. 648.

[122] *CSP* Domestic 136 (1547-80): p. 648. From it Corro must have been at Court with the Earl.

[123] Mc Fadden deduces as much from the payment books' evidence, cited in note 116 above; see also pp. 496 n. 2.

[124] *BW* 3: p. 73; Diocesan Registry, Reg: Grindal, folio 204 (from McFadden, p. 512 n. 2) describes him as a " naturalized Englishman."

[125] John Le Neve, *Fasti ecclesiae Anglicanae* (Oxford, 1854) 1: p. 601.

[126] Printed in Hessels 2: pp. 667-75.

[127] Wood 2 i: pp. 197-98; Curtis, pp. 213-23.

[128] Curtis, pp. 213-23.

[129] *Kerk. St.*, pp. 227-28 on these 1618 editions; see also Curtis, pp. 211-12; *GN* 3: p. 184; Porter, p. 283; *BW* 3: p. 77; L. Knappert, *Het Onstaan en de Vestiging van het Protestantisme in de Nederlanden* (Utrecht, 1924): p. 367 and n. 1 for a discussion of Arminianism in this context.

[130] *CSP* Spanish 3: p. 166 which is Mendoza's report. He calls Corro a " professor of writing."

131 Gustav Ungerer, *Anglo-Spanish Relations in Tudor Literature* (Bern-Madrid, 1956): pp. 69-70. This book covers far more valuable grounds for historians than its title perhaps suggests. See also *BW* 3: pp. 73-74; McFadden cites a long Latin letter from Corro to Jean Hotman on p. 517 n. 1.

132 See note 10 above.

133 Corrado Vivanti, *Lotta politica e Pace religiosa in Francia fra cinque e seicento* (Turin, 1963), reviewed by Frances Yates in *History* 50 (June, 1965): pp. 223-24.

134 *CSP* Foreign Elizabeth 15: p. 520; *GN* 3: pp. 179-80. On Pucci see note 101 above.

135 Wood 2 i; pp. 210-11; *BW* 3: p. 73. Leicester's letter is cited in full by McFadden, p. 513 and n. 2.

136 *Ibid.* and McFadden's full quote on p. 514 and n. 1.

137 *BW* 3: p. 74.

138 Same as note 137 above. Porter, p. 283 suggests that Travers's attack on the two men was a " compliment " to both !

139 McFadden, pp. 526 ff has a detailed exposition on Corro's last years in these personal matters which is more than adequate, and which is unnecessary to go into for our purposes.

140 McFadden, p. 537 n. 1 has noticed the cessation of the relevant payments; see also *BW* 3: pp. 75-76; *GN* 3: pp. 182-83.

141 Ungerer, p. 168.

242 McFadden, p. 557 n. 2 has, with customary industry, searched out Corro's resting place.

IV. CONCLUSIONS

In the aforementioned article on Pucci in England Firpo concluded his analysis of Corro by observing that " despite a penchant for Calvinism Corro was a free thinker." [1] While we are reluctant to call him a " free thinker " it is indisputable that through approximately 1570 Corro certainly possessed an almost untraceable " penchant for Calvinism." Perhaps if we divest the term free thinker of its usual connotations it fits; undisciplined or independent, however, seems more accurate for Corro during and after his adherence to Geneva. Our amending of Fruin's designation of the Spaniard from " Evangelical Christian " to " Evangelical Calvinist " for the years 1555-70 may prove useful for categorizing, insofar as that is needed. Corro carried his increasingly irenical tendencies, derived primarily from his recondite readings at San Isidro and his experiences at Montargis, into Anglicanism, to all appearances. The struggles with the Strangers' Churches, exacerbated by Theodore Beza's letters brought out his latent anti-reprobationist proclivities. One of the amusing ironies characterizing Corro throughout his travails was the odd combination of his doctrinal and ethical appeals for charity, faith, good deeds, and the love of God and Christ with a hot temper, irreverent tongue and pen, and willingness on occasion to descend to tactics which enraged him when utilized by his opponents. Perhaps the psychologically-oriented student would interpret this as a form of compensation; while tempting, however, such an approach is outside our scope and competence, and psychoanalyzing the dead, not to mention the living, is never easy. And whether or not it is just to reduce religious experiences to solely emotional phenomena raises another host of matters, not directly relevant here.

The geographical sweep of Corro's life—from Andalusia to Oxford—strikes the imagination as fertile ground for what we called in the introduction a " grassroots " insight into Reformation years. His amazing range of friends and enemies reenforces the possibilities and opportunities inherent in this approach. We hope that others will see fit to undertake similar endeavors with men like Juan Pérez and Adrian Saravia,[2] even if they were not quite as " fantastic " as our subject.

[1] Firpo, " Pucci in Inghilatera," p. 169 f.

[2] Adrian Saravia, born in Hesdin in Artois of Spanish parentage, was equally as fascinating as Corro, although there seems to be less material extant on him. He played very important roles in the Low Countries and England. The only study of him at all is Jean Meyerhoff, " Adrien Saravia " BSHP Belge Series 2 (July, 1921): pp. 66-74. See our Appendix on him.

PART II

THE OTHERS

I. CASSIODORO DE REINA
(c. 1520 - 94)

Only Cassiodoro de Reina's career and writings provoked as much controversy, and indeed as much contemporary and subsequent confusion, as Corro's. Like the latter and Cypriano de Valera he was a product of the curiously heretical milieu of San Isidro and Seville, and he appears to have fled Spain to Geneva at the same time as his fellow Hieronymites.[1] His role in London, to be considerably expounded on in this chapter, and his futile meeting in Orleans with Des Gallars and Corro have previously been noted.[2] Reina, it should be remarked at once, possesses significance in that his Bible was the continuation of earlier endeavors by Enzinas and Juan Pérez, and the foundation for Valera's Castilian Bible, to be discussed in the next chapter.

For a brief time he directed the tiny Spanish congregation in Geneva.[3] For reasons unknown he migrated to Frankfurt in 1558 where he joined the French Calvinist Church.[4] Beyond such bare details we know virtually nothing about Reina's early years until his emergence in the refugee community in London; as in similar cases Elizabeth's accession inspired his removal to that city.[5] There also is some indication that he was in dire poverty in Frankfurt, which could easily account for his exodus.[6] In this regard it is again necessary to stress the heroism behind such journeys, even if taken through largely Protestant territories. While I have commented on the initial collective courage of the San Isidrians' escape, it is useful to quote Tollin here: " The Spanish Inquisition occupied all roads from Geneva [north] to Cologne, Frankfurt..., Antwerp... and [south] to Milan and

Venice." [7] The examples of Juan Diaz a generation before, and the San Isidrian Juan de Leon, testified grimly to the persistence of the Holy Office and Philip II's diplomatic-espionage apparatus. No single, seemingly insignificant Spanish heretic could appear to the latter as not worth pursuing, within or without Spanish territorial jurisdiction. For loyal Spanish Catholics such cases were an affront to the national honor, as well as the Lord's.[8]

I have dealt previously with the general situations of the refugee Calvinist Strangers' Churches in London under Edward VI and Elizabeth, up to and including the collapse of the Spanish one in 1565.[9] At the time I submitted that notice I did not have access to Reina's Confession of Faith for his congregation, composed possibly in collaboration with Valera, early in 1559. It is high irony that in the " Author's Letter to the Reader " which opened the 1577 edition it was claimed that this work succeeded in its primary intention of allowing the Spaniards to live in peace and communion with their co-religionnaires.[10] As I indicated in the earlier study the Confession had precisely the opposite effect, at least among the influential leaders of the French Church (to which Reina had belonged briefly on his arrival in London), despite Bishop Grindal's approval and the indeterminate acquiescence of the other Strangers' Churches in the capitol. It is almost amusing to consider the range of reactions to this document, which had so pacific an aim. The French rejected its statement on baptism and ultimately the entire work; not till later were they to discover other grounds for assaulting its author (but never Valera, curiously, assuming he was a junior colleague in its composition).[11] At the Colloquy of Poissy in 1561 which Reina attended through the generosity of Throgmorton, the English ambassador to France, his Confession was charged with " crypto-Lutheranism." [12] More recently it has been labelled as professing " doctrines common to all Protestants, but as to the Eucharist [was] Reformed... not Lutheran "; partially " Servetian "; and combining the 42 Articles of Cranmer and the Augusburg Confession.[13]

Without going farther, and perhaps wildly afield, recently I obtained a copy of the 1601 bi-lingual edition of Reina's Confession.[14] Chapter XII (Of Baptism) treats the initial bone of contention between the author and the London French. In section I he commented that infant baptism was an " institution " ordered by God which carried out his benefice and gave testimony at the same time of faith in Christ. These themes were amplified in the remainder of this part.[15] In section 3 lies undoubtedly the pandora's box which commenced Reina's theological and other subsequent hardships. For here he noted the absence of any express scriptural mention of children's baptism before the age of reason. Nonetheless, he hurried on, he held with the Church of God that it is better to admit than forbid this sacrament which pertained to God's covenants.[16] To the embattled defenders of orthodox Calvinism such a quasi-rationalist, philological admission concerning one of the fundamentals of the faith was a horrifying surrender of the fortress of irreducible dogma, and a clear sign of the impending, if not actual heterodoxy of its author. Indeed, Reina here took his first step towards becoming a classic illustration of the theses of Febvre and Walzer put forth in the introduction.

To recapitulate my previous account of Reina and his church's development, suffice it to note that between 1559 and 1563 no difficulties arose. Then, in rapid order came the Queen's wrath at his marriage and the Balthazar Sánchez deposition against him, with its incredible array of charges.[17] The real tragedy, of course, lay in what seems fair to call Reina's cowardice under fire. He was not lacking ardent defenders, Bishop Grindal among them. Yet he undercut them, his congregation, and ultimately his family and himself by his sudden, clandestine flight to the continent before any formal hearing, much less a decision, could be held to determine the accusations' validity. In all fairness, however, Elizabeth's violent reaction to Reina's marriage just before the storm broke may very well have persuaded him that there could be no check on his enemies and no fair process.[18] It is hard, though, to imagine Corro not merely bowing before such an attack, but leaving committed supporters in the lurch. It was precisely the opportunity that Reina's precipitate departure created which the French Consistory seized to impound the Théobon note, as we have seen. One wonders if Corro were fully aware of this some months later in France.

The astoundingly contradictory moral accusations aside,[19] it is imperative to examine Reina's belief as stated in the 1559 Confession with respect to the general suggestion by his opponents that somehow he was an anti-Trinitarian. In Chapter I (Of God), section 2 he observed that to God the Father " the Christ [was] His eternal Word... the natural portrait and expressed image of the person of the Father... the Holy Spirit the force and efficacy of the divinity which shows itself generally in all God's works, and most clearly in the government of all the churches of Jesus Christ..."[20] In section 3 he pronounced his belief (and therefore his congregation's) in the " three persons in the same substance [and] nature... of God..." without their separation prejudicing or lessening the " unity and simplicity of one God..."[21] Section 4 declared that human reason could not attain and fathom mysteries of the kind just outlined, but that men must follow the Fathers and their faith in such matters. Finally, the fifth section of this key chapter railed against " ancient and modern sects that denied the distinction of the [three] Persons within the unity of the divine nature..."[22]

I suggest that Reina was an orthodox Calvinist on the Trinity, as well as on infant baptism, despite his tendency to be very literal concerning scriptural justification for the latter; at least as of this, and several subsequent writings. Rather, he was one of numerous victims to the growing " theological furor," which phenomenon is all too frequently assigned solely to post-Luther Lutheranism in this period. Indeed, his accusers were in the ranks of Febvre's " sincere " rhetoricians of dogma, many of whom figured prominently in the lives of Corro and Saravia. Perhaps they should have forseen that their wish, or belief about such persons, eventually contained a larger element of truth than originally, as the accused gradually or suddenly (in Saravia's case) recoiled from Calvinism in face of such exaggerated attack.

The third major area of controversy concerning Reina's theology was his view of the Eucharist, which, as noted, brought forth an impressive array of mutually contradictory opinions.

In Chapter XIII (On Holy Communion), section 1, he wrote that it should be " legitimately administered with true faith... in memory of the Lord's death... [according to ancient and apostolic usage] " and that " the bread [was] the same and true body of the Lord who gave Himself up to death for us, and the wine His own blood which was shed to pardon our sins, conforming to [His] words: 'Take [this bread and wine], this is my body, this is my blood." [23] Indeed, so far, this could be viewed as a Lutheran position. Section 2 observed that this " Sacrament [is the] certain and firm testimony of God that those admitted to His new covenant... are spiritually sustained and maintained by [it], with the sustenance of His body and blood in order to likewise participate in His divine and eternal life, being incorporated in Him... through His flesh and blood." [24] Lastly, section 3 proclaimed that the adherents of this new covenant " in whose hearts God has written His law " would show " pure piety and sanctity... through singular charity, love, and union " wherever and with whomever they might be.[25]

I believe that this entire chapter lends itself to a Lutheran interpretation, despite the passing notice of the sacrament being " in memory of the Lord's death " in the opening section. However, it was preceded by Chapter XI (Of the Sacraments of the Christian Church), which in section 1 declared that the sacraments " confirm[ed] the benefaction of our salvation and fulfillment of [Christ's] promises: we receive these through faith..." [26] The ensuing section seems to me at the very least, non-Lutheran, if not broadly Reformed. Here the sacraments are defined as " the external means or instruments through which we apply to ourselves this benefaction..." [27] while section 3 reduces them to Baptism and the Eucharist alone.[28] Several years later Reina removed any possibility of attributing a quasi-Lutheran coloring to his position on the Eucharist when he called the bread and the wine symbols and also specifically adopted Calvin's view that infidels could partake in this ceremony.[29]

Reina left England sometime during the winter of 1563-64, and turned up briefly in Antwerp, where his family soon joined him.[30] Sometime following the abortive meeting at Orleans he moved to hospitable Frankfurt.[31] Early in 1565 he was approached by the French (Calvinist) Strangers' Church of Strasbourg with a view towards his assuming the ministry there.[32] Presumably this Consistory either had not heard of his seeming disgrace in London, or had good reason to ignore that complex situation. The congregation, however, apparently did consult several leading Calvinist divines about Reina's credentials; the hostile joint testimony of three is extant.[33] From their letter, which was based on an interview with Reina, Olevianus and his brethren expressed grave doubts over the Spaniard's views on the Eucharist, Christ's ascension, and His position at God's right hand. It was in response to this attack, obviously communicated to him by the Strasbourgers, that Reina penned an amplification of his positions as outlined from the 1559 Confession. Interestingly, Olevianus claimed that Reina had told them he had fled England because six sworn witnesses had deposed against him, morally and doctrinally; under the second rubric was the deadly charge of Servetianism.[34] If all this were true it seems particularly depressing that Reina lacked the courage to stand by Chapters I and VIII of the Confession which most assuredly clear him of anti-Trinitarianism, as even his interlocutors admitted he denied these accusations. The tone of the Olevianus note exudes distrust of Reina and the assumption that all charges made against him in London probably were true; in sum, like Corro, he was guilty until proven innocent.

In his lengthy letter to the Strasbourg congregation defending himself, Reina quoted Martin Bucer to some extent to protest against ubiquitarianism, while simultaneously insisting that Christ's ascension was " exempt from local conditions." Not only is Christ enclosed by no one place, but to inquire further into how He is situated in the heavens strikes Reina as impious and presumptuous. For him it is enough to say that Christ lives inaccessibly and gloriously with God His Father, but He has given us the Eucharist, which series of ideas follows logically enough from the notion that basically such matters are " incomprehensible to human reason " and are to be held by faith.[35] A goodly portion of the letter sketched the eucharistic differences among the major Reformers, which Reina adroitly used to suggest none of these eminences could be called heretics by any stretch of the imagination; in fact, he chastized Luther alone for his violence in this regard, despite his undoubted greatness. He concluded with a carefully enumerated self-defence, and in passing, weakly said he left London to better employ his time and talents than waste them in such debates. This, however, with the rest of this " petite " confession of faith satisfied the people of Strasbourg.[36]

It failed to satisfy others. Beza declared that Reina still "appeared to be too much of a Lutheran," while Olevianus remained an implacable enemy.[37]   On January 28, 1566 Reina wrote a second, much shorter notice for general consumption, apparently, since it was not addressed specifically to any party.[38] This began with the concession that his prior statement of March, 1565 may well have contained seeming contradictions and the like (this presumably does not apply to the more detailed 1559 document), and Reina consented to summarize and clarify his positions. In the interim his remark that in the Eucharist Christ was " *presentialement* and *sustantialement* " had aroused some warm debate. Here he contended that he meant only the perception of the Saviour's divine spirit and virtues through faith in communion, not by a corporeal presence. In passing he noted that by using such terminology he had hoped to effect a reconciliation with the Germans (Lutherans), which, perhaps, foreshadowed his more hospitable reception in Lutheran circles in Strasbourg and elsewhere and his subsequent conversion to that faith.   The brief apology ended with a scripturally-reinforced reworking of his initial observations on the ubiquitarian issues.[39]

Since the foregoing was sent from Frankfurt it is clear Reina did not accept the proffered post at Strasbourg, the congregation's apparent support notwithstanding. In the brief testimonial from the latter appended to the March 24, 1565 confession the signatories noted that it was only at Reina's own insistence that he defer their offer until such time as he was exonerated of the charges from London which caused them to look elsewhere. It

91

is also probable that Reina felt his presence as a minister would damage the Strasbourg Church, given Beza and Olevianus's unrelenting enmity to him. Considering the problem of the testimonial's genuineness I am inclined to leave that matter aside. Whatever the case, Reina stayed on at Frankfurt, although he made occasional trips to Strasbourg to visit friends like Johan Sturm, and to Basel in connection with the Bible project. By June, 1568 he had moved to the latter.[40]

Adolf Fluri has analyzed the complicated character of the negotiations with the printers, indeed the rather grave finances of the matter which attended Reina personally, as well as the successful—and important—outcome of the project.[41] Marcus Pérez, who had exiled himself to Basel with the triumph of Spanish forces in the Low Countries in March, 1567, and two eminent Lutherans of Basel, Simon Sulzer and Huldrich Köchlein, assisted him during the trying final stages of publication.[42] Although Reina's transference to Lutheranism was approximately a decade off, he spoke admiringly of the Augsburg Confession in his Bible's dedicatory letter.[43]

The following year, 1570, Reina and his family returned to Frankfurt. His Bible's appearance failed to make life easier. On occasion he worked as a laborer, although, curiously, he also taught for leading Jewish families.[44] Just before the departure from Basel Johan Sturm wrote directly to Queen Elizabeth on his behalf, defending Reina as a man victimized by calumny and guiltless of the old accusations. He portrayed the Spaniard as still faithful to England and desirious of having an edition of the new Bible printed under her auspices " if he [Reina] thought the Spaniards would suffer it without resentment." On September 8 Sturm repeated this request to Cecil, and soon after Reina followed with an application to the latter for aid.[45] These appeals went ignored, helped no doubt by the recent (1568) formal denunciation of Reina by the London French Church for his " impurities " and disappearance from the country while under suspicion.[46] Once more Reina and his friends had cause to regret that precipitous flight. But " rehabilitation " remained out of reach, at least for the present and the forseeable future.

Reina rejoined the French Church at Frankfurt, news of which reinvigorated the predictable ire of Theodore Beza, the major bitter-end antagonist of the Spanish Protestant heterodox, so it seemed. A three-way exchange of letters involving Reina, Beza, and the Frankfurt Consistory ensued, ending in Reina's acceptance by the congregation to Beza's considerable disgust.[47] That Calvin's successor failed to sway this church suggests limits to his presumed powers of arbitration and authority. On the other hand it is false to stress congregational autonomy from the Genevan doctors in such an episode. Rather, the paramount factor here probably was the local Calvinists, both as refugees and non-Lutherans, had to tread cautiously in Reina's case, especially since he rapidly obtained citizenship of the city.[48] A. A. Van Schelven has recounted the particularly brutal attack Olevianus subjected Reina to at this time, in the course of his reply to a local minister's query about the Spaniard. His language typified the vitriolic, personal nature of such situations.[49] It was during this altercation that Reina professed he " had never claimed to apply [Bucer] against... the Confession of the Reformed Churches of France and Switzerland..." whereas in 1565 he had called him " a man worthy of immortal memory."[50] Of course the former statement left the door open to use Bucer's doctrines against Olevianus's Heidelberg Confession, if need be, which was undoubtedly more to the point in Frankfurt; but in view of Reina's frequent use of and homage to Bucer this smacks of a certain hypocrisy.

Comparatively speaking Reina spent the years 1571-78 in quiet obscurity.[51] In 1577 he was, however, offered a ministerial post in Poland which he declined for unknown reasons.[52] Then from Antwerp, after the conclusion of the religious peace agreed upon there on July 22, 1578, Reina was invited by the French-Walloon Lutheran congregation to be its pastor. The precise sequence of events eludes the student,[53] but it is plausible to think that now Reina felt it absolutely necessary to be cleared formally of the old London charges. Indeed, such vindication would be doubly mandatory for a still controversial Calvinist who proposed to renounce that faith in order to become a

Lutheran leader in an explosively Calvinist region; one wonders, too, if he recalled that once in the Low Countries Philip II's price on his head would undoubtedly be renewed, if in fact it had ever been formally abandoned.

Clearly he did not hesitate to accept the proffered post. He arrived in London late that year where a hearing was rapidly commenced to bring to a head the unresolved business of fifteen years' duration. Mendoza, the Spanish ambassador to England, noted that Reina's " passport " was important letters from his old friend Sturm for the Queen's Council.[54] This in itself could have only done him good in English eyes. In this report Mendoza also observed that Reina was " being favored by some of the principal people here." Suffice it to comment that Grindal, now Archbishop of Canterbury, never seems to have changed his basically favorable outlook on Reina, which contrasts directly with the nature of his feelings towards Corro. Mendoza also said that Reina was agitating for the restoration of an autonomous Spanish Church, which of course failed to develop. In a subsequent letter home he added that " the heretic... has been boasting... of having brought hither a number of Spanish Bibles he had printed in Germany to send to Spain." [55] Undoubtedly the growing overtly anti-Spanish atmosphere in the country, abetted by Mendoza's own lack of diplomatic finesse, aided Reina in his impending "rehabilitation," his imminent Lutheranism regardless. This, obviously, was a far cry from the early 1560's when Elizabeth often took great pains to assuage her one-time brother-in-law.[56]

The commission of inquiry, headed by Grindal, was entirely English, in marked contrast to most of those concerning Corro. There is no evidence, incidentally, that the two Spaniards ever communicated or met at this time, although Cypriano de Valera stepped forward on Reina's behalf.[57] While sending out letters of inquiry about Reina to various personages on the continent the commission rapidly dismissed all personal and moral charges as groundless.[58] The varying opinions were speedily collated. By March, 1579 it was announced that Reina was innocent of all doctrinal accusations, excepting a certain weakness on infant baptism, which, it was graciously noted, was easily corrected.[59] His work on the Bible was recalled favorably, which contrasts ironically with the unsuccessful earlier attemps by Sturm and himself in that respect.[60] This decision shattered, rightly I believe, the long-standing charges of Servetianism and that Reina was somehow heretical in his treatment of the Eucharist and related matters. However, while the Walloon Calvinist Churches of Antwerp and Frankfurt, Reina's future neighbor and past community respectively, expressed their complete acceptance of these findings,[61] the London French Consistory, apparently backed by the equally intransigent Beza, remained adamant; Reina's last confrontation with it on March 22 proved mutually fruitless.[62] Indeed its repudiation of the Grindal commission's decision on Reina must have weakened them subsequently vis-à-vis Corro, who proved unassailable in broadly similar circumstances during the 1580's. This affair also may have helped prepare the ground for the rejection of Beza (politely) by Whitgift and others in the ' 90's.

Despite what I have said about the worsening character of Anglo-Spanish relations and its indirect bearing on the Reina affair it is clear that his acquittal affected orthodox Calvinism, and possibly the Puritans, far more than Catholic Spain. As much is plainly suggested by the vindictive reactions of the London French, while the Spaniards ceased paying specific attention to the matter. Corro's career in these years and afterwards also points in a similar direction on the whole, probably even more so. These episodes in both men's lives prepared the way, in a sense, for Saravia in the 1590's and the growing English Arminian protest against certain aspects of Calvinism, such as reprobation, adhered to firmly by the Strangers' Churches and the Puritans.

I suspect also that those Calvinists, such as the Frankfurt congregation, and moderates like Sturm may have been undercut by Reina's immediate turn to Lutheranism, which conversion resembled Saravia's to Anglicanism in its sudden blitheness. The previous protestations of men like Beza and Olevianus that Reina and his ilk were untrustworthy hypocrites seemed to be now borne out to Calvinists. As we shall see, however, Reina steered himself and his Lutheran community very astutely in a Calvinist milieu.

It remains to glance at the London articles signed by Reina on March 19, 1579.[63] The two brief introductory sections are quite confusing. The first stated: " Confession of Cassiodorus Reina, Spanish minister in the Church on the particular subject of the Lord's Supper, which Augustan Confession he himself delivered at Antwerp, which Confession if his colleagues in the priesthood will sincerely profess, will remove the controversy among them and among the ministers of the Reformed Churches." This suggests several puzzling possibilities: that he went to Antwerp where he subscribed formally to the Augsburg Confession before going to London for his hearing; [64] that within the ranks of the local Lutherans as well as between them and the Calvinists continued to run bitter eucharistic quarrels. But the second " preface " read: " *Confession of Cassiodorus Reina:* I,... Reina, Spanish citizen (a most striking remark, reminding one of Corro's stubborn ' Spanishness, which in a sense shows the reverse side of Philip's continuing to regard them all as his subjects) and minister... at Frankfurt, permit to be read this Confession of Faith of the Churches of Switzerland, in order that it may be in like manner orthodox and conforming to the Word of God, and to the Confession I subscribe my soul and my all..." In two short paragraphs Reina presented himself as adhering to the Augsburg and Swiss Confessions, while simultaneously calling himself pastor at Antwerp and Frankfurt. I cannot resolve these contradictions very concretely... However, Lehnemann copied the lost originals in the early eighteenth century for a work which concentrated on Reina's career as a Lutheran minister in Frankfurt and Antwerp. Is it plausible to believe he unwittingly erred in having Reina call himself a minister at Frankfurt prematurely,[65] as it were ? Certainly it was hardly likely that the Spaniard would have announced in print that he had just subscribed to the Augsburg Confession in the process of trying, with English assistance, to appease the Calvinists by signing " Swiss " articles of reconciliation. Unless, of course,

Reina simply no longer cared what happened after he obtained "clearance" from London concerning Calvinist opinion about him; that, however, would seem to presuppose on his part at least a strong feeling the Grindal panel was going to acquit him. Ultimately no one really knows.

The five articles extant (I do not know if there were more) all concern the Eucharist. The first of these asked about "the Meaning of the Words of the Supper and whether [these] ought to be understood literally or figuratively?" Reina replied that "they ought to be taken figuratively, unless we wish to confuse the sign with things themselves figuratively... And so, I feel that... the bread ought to signify... the body of Christ, and the wine, His blood." Article II concerned "Whether the body of Christ is really and corporeally present...?" and the reply was: "Reverently and substantially [it is] present. [But] it is consumed... neither corporeally nor physically... neither of the body nor the flesh, but entirely of the spirit." To Article III which asked if the body and blood was to be eaten orally the Spaniard answered that they were in fact food for the soul alone and therefore were consumed "mentally and through true faith, since they are outside of all physical conditions," even though "chewed in the mouth" as bread and wine. The penultimate article very briefly restated the third; the last queried Reina about banning the impious from this sacrament. He declared: "I feel so. But they who love the true faith should by no means be judged more prepared for the sacred deed than pigs and dogs, unless they are free of all sin; otherwise they abuse the holiest things. Therefore those who receive the sacrament in... sin receive as an indifferent pig... would..." This last strikes me as a long-delayed strong retort to his numerous enemies, so quick to exclude him from Christian communities, their own lives presumably regardless. At the end of this final reply Reina submitted directly to Archbishop Grindal that if "certain words... fail to express the true and genuine sense of these things, [they] may be freely corrected." Clearly he recalled his earlier difficulties arising from ambiguities in his style and terminology, and this clause seemed expressedly designed to be a broad interpretive safety-valve. Whether or not it indeed appeased all his ancient antagonists may be doubted.

On the face of these articles Reina should have been able to reestablish his reputation in Calvinist circles, as in some instances cited it apparently was, if temporarily. But entrenched hostility in others, the ambiguous loophole concluding the articles, and most damagingly and obviously, his immediate adhesion to Lutheranism as a minister plainly explained why on the whole Reina remained an object of derision, even fear, among many Calvinists, English good-will notwithstanding. Added irony came shortly after he joined his new congregation when some of its ultra-conservative members branded him as a " crypto-Calvinist " on the basis of these five articles ! [66] However, this attack lacked meaningful support and gave Reina no real trouble.

Potentially the Netherlandish Lutherans were in great danger around 1580, not only from Parma's armies. The Calvinists, spurred on by preachers like Dathenus and Hembyze, were reviving the violent spirit of the 1566 *saccagements* (iconoclastic riots) against Catholics, which despite Orange's countervailing efforts were rapidly alienating the Catholic nobility. This " fury " could easily have been directed at the Lutherans, too, inspired perhaps by the memory of the latter community's diffidence in 1566-67,[67] as well as the awareness of Lutheran persecution of fellow Calvinists in areas like the Palatinate during 1576-83. Reina's aversions from further religious strife coincided with local conditions, however, to produce a politique approach to the ruling faith. One interesting case suffices to illustrate: just after Reina's arrival Orange's chaplain, Corro's old Oxford opponent, Loiseleur de Villiers, was pilloried by the ultra-Flaccian party in Antwerp.[68] The new paster's conciliatory handling of this delicate matter, which might have resulted in even the Orangists attacking the Lutherans, earned Villiers's respect and sympathy, at least for Reina personally. That, in turn, helped to assure the latter's church a tranquil existence in this hotly Calvinist region. In fact, the conservatives within his own congregation provided Reina with the only remotely difficult time he experienced in his six years at Antwerp.[69]

Aside, then, from occasional unfriendly reminders from other Lutherans of his previous Calvinism and subscription to the " Swiss " articles of 1579, Reina and this community were on the whole sheltered both from the intransigent Calvinism of the Low Countries and the growing theological furor which was rending Lutheranism in Germany.[70] Naturally, however, Parma's conquest of the city in 1585 altered conditions drastically. For such a time his offer to all Protestants of four years' grace before they had to quit Antwerp or convert to Catholicism was most generous. Some of Reina's flock had already removed to Frankfurt, where Reina and most of the rest soon joined them. For our purposes his return there is of little concern.[71] Suffice it to note that the Senate, which had previously shown him favor as a Calvinist in the 1570's, pursued a policy towards all the refugee congregations which may be summed up as Germanization and Lutheranization.[72] Curiously, Reina himself ended not merely as a successful minister and noted biblicist, but also as a remarkably prosperous entrepreneur.[73]

Finally, it remains to examine briefly Reina's last known utterance, a statement he made to his congregation on May 8, 1593.[74] He proclaimed firstly his adherence to the Augsburg and Wittenberg Confessions, the Schmalkaldic Articles, the Lutheran Catechism, the " Agreement of Bucer established among the ministers of the city in the 42nd year, and the Book of the Agreement of the 82nd year recently drawn up by the Protestant States..." Secondly Reina affirmed his belief that all heresies and errors outlined in J. Andreae's *Formula of Concord* were indeed " impious, fanatical, and contrary to the Word of God..." Among these he included Catholicism, Anabaptism, the Flaccian Lutherans, and Sacramentarians, both Zwinglian and Calvinist. Thirdly, he subscribed without reservation to the Lutheran view of the Eucharist as recently clarified by Andrææ. Fourthly, Reina discussed the 1579 Articles, echoes of which still apparently came back to him in the Lutheran milieu. He pointed out in the course of " exhibiting " them at this occasion that he had not signed them in the London French Church, which he deemed " important." He said the " judges [had] not sought from me

99

a complete confession on the Lord's Supper, since it was given in a few certain previous articles." I take this last to refer to his earlier statements on the subject, such as the 1559 Confession. This also implies the 1579 articles covered nothing else. Reina must have been aware his casuistry here was, at the least, devious both to Lutherans and Calvinists, for he pleaded: " I swear honestly and before God that I have thought about this [the 1579 articles] both inside and outside of judgment and after I had departed from England: that I have acted in the fullness of faith before all, I have not been a Calvinist (!)..." After further such self-abasement, Reina ended this rather tortuous section by placing himself and his doctrines in the hands of the audience, whom he exhorted to judge him by his life since 1579, while he expressed his characteristic willingness to have anything contrary to his present beliefs brought into conformity with the current Lutheran creed.[75]

Reina is perhaps more difficult to assess than even Corro. Outwardly the latter is more admirable in that he fought adversity head-on. By comparison, too, Corro's reasons for converting to Anglicanism appear quite clear; whereas Reina's motive for joining Lutheranism at the moment he was signing very non-Lutheran pronouncements may well been an overpowering desire to end his poverty, become a minister, and indicate his profound disdain of Calvinism, however pettily. Had he turned away from the latter just after his flight from London in 1563-64 the matter would have been understandable. Reina, in fact, was characterized by a weakness and deviousness unthinkable in Corro, despite the second man's occasional tactical underhandedness. In very similar situations Reina ran or prevaricated. Corro stood fast and gave in return, and much more openly.

It may not be right to evaluate Reina negatively alongside Corro. In his Bible he made an enduring contribution to the Hispanic and Protestant worlds. Corro's significance must be measured were in terms of scattered personal impact. Both men shared in the emerging reaction to certain aspects of orthodox Calvinism, as particularly enumerated in the chapters on Corro. Saravia, for apparently very differing reasons, was to inherit this in part later in the century, well after Reina had become an open Lutheran and Corro an aging Angican. To him we turn after a brief glance at Cypriano de Valera, the completer of Reina's Bible, and the sole individual in this quartet who did not come to reject his youthful Calvinism.

---

[1] McFadden, 54.

[2] For the London years see my *Church History* article cited frequently in Pt. I of this study; for the Orleans meeting see *ibid.*, ch. 2, notes pp. 52-55.

[3] Schickler, 1: p. 122.

[4] A. A. Van Schelven, "Cassiodorus de Reyna, Christophorus Fabricius en Gaspar Olevianus," *Nederlandsch Archief voor Kerkgeschiedenis*, 8 (1911): p. 323 f; *BW*, 2: p. 165.

[5] One of those supposed details is worth passing comment. Many contemporary Spanish authorities and agents considered Reina of Morisco origin, which, of course, was an added disgrace in their eyes. This seems baseless, however. See *BW*, 2: p. 171 and n. 21.

[6] Johannes Lehnemann, *Historische Nachricht von der Evangelisch Lutherischen Kirche in Antorff* (Frankfurt, 1725): p. 92 ff. Its ancient age notwithstanding this book is invaluable for the story of Reina and his congregation in Antwerp and Frankfurt during 1579-1594 in particular.

[7] Henri Tollin, "Cassiodoro de Reina," *BSHPF*, 21 (1882): p. 389.

[8] E.g. my *Historical Journal* article cited frequently in Pt. I.

[9] Hauben, "A Spanish Calvinist Church."

[10] I have not seen this edition. It is quoted in *BW*, 2: p. 167 and n. 13.

[11] *HSP*, 38: pp. xx, 13, 23, 26, 29, 35; *BW*, 2: p. 167 and n. 13.

[12] Tollin, 31: p. 397; Van Lennep, p. 358 f.

[13] Respectively John Stoughton, *The Spanish Reformers* (London, 1883): p. 296; Tollin, 31: p. 390 f; Lieselotte Linnhoff, *Spanische Protestanten und England* (Emsdetten, 1934): p. 35. None of these three strike me as very reliable students of the subject generally, it should be added. Lehnemann, p. 92 n. 4, who is far superior in his evaluations believed that Reina's version of the Eucharist at this time alienated most Calvinists; see notes 23 ff below.

[14] Thanks to the kindness of Dr. J. Dietze, Director of the Landesbibliothek of the University of Sachsen-Anhalt in Halle, I obtained a

microfilm copy of this edition in (apparently) the original Spanish, with a parallel German translation, which I have donated to the New-berry Library, Chicago. This was brought out by one Eberhardten von Retrodt, who presumably did the German column, and who was captain of the castle guard at Cassel for the Prince of Hesse-Cassel. Wilhelm Wessel was the printer. The Spanish version begins with undoubtedly the original date, January 4, 1559. All citations follow the original folio pagination. Some of the introductory and concluding sections were missing, as well as fol. G—Giiij from the Confession itself. The above-mentioned library at Halle, as well as several others in that part of East Germany, do not to my knowledge have more data relevant to this field. I spent some time there in August, 1966, and wish here to record my gratitude to Dr. Dietze and his most obliging staff, Pastor Kuhn for showing me through the private Marienkirche collection in Halle, and Professor Arno Lehmann of the Martin Luther University, Halle-Wittenberg for his general kindness to a visitor, professionally and socially.

[15] Fol. D-Dij.

[16] Fol. Dij-Diij.

[17] Hauben, "A Spanish Calvinist Church," p. 53. As Reina was not, however, specifically charged with any deviation regarding predesti-nation at this time I have omitted a discussion of chs. 20-21 in the 1559 Confession which deal, quite Calvinistically, with that matter. The same holds for the March, 1565 letter discussed below. See Valera ch. for another instance of Elizabeth's profound dislike of married clergy.

[18] BW, 2: pp. 171 and n. 23.

[19] See Hauben, "A Spanish Calvinist Church," p. 53; these included simultaneous adultery and sodomy with members of the same family.

[20] Retrodt ed., fol. Aiiij-Av. " Portrait " seems to mean here copy or resemblance, and " expressed " could also be taken as clear or purposeful. Given the climate of the day one wonders if somehow the seemingly innocuous phrase, " all the churches of Jesus Christ " could have been misconstrued as embracing non-Calvinist Christianity.

[21] Fol. Av.

[22] Fol. Av. In ch. 8 (On the Nature and Person of Christ) he wrote: " We believe... Christ in his nature and person to be true man... [and]... true God since in his person and substance is the Word..." fol. Bv. Calvin also stressed man's inability to penetrate mysteries such as these in the last analysis, E.g. Calvin: On the Christian Faith, John T. McNeill, ed. (NY-Indianapolis, 1957, paper ed.): pp. 118 ff. This is a very useful selection from his major writings. Cf. n. 35 below.

[23] Fol. Diij.

[24] Fol. Diij.

[25] Fol. Diij-Diiij.

[26] Fol. Cv.

[27] Fol. Cv.

[28] Fol. Cv-D.

[29] This letter is reprinted in *BW*, 2: pp. 194-201; the original can be consulted at Geneva in the Musée de la Réformation, Corr. Eccl. Mss. fr. 407 v. 7, which is a volume consecrated solely to letters involving Reina and Corro from 1565-71. Perhaps I should observe that this " should have " removed any legitimacy from a Lutheran taint; reality, as we have noted throughout this study, did not necessarily follow logic, common-sense or otherwise.

[30] *BW*, 2 :p. 171 f and notes 21, 22, and 27. Marcus Pérez, his later benefactor at Basel, gave the Reina family shelter and necessities.

[31] *BW*, 2: p. 173 says early in 1565, but that appears to presume a longer stay at Antwerp than probable, given the Spanish price on his head once the authorities learned of his presence there. Of course, the Orleans meeting was followed by Reina's brief stay at Montargis with Corro.

[32] *Ibid.*, 2: p. 173, based on Olevianus's remarks in his letter attacking Reina, printed there on pp. 192-93, says Beza's recommendation motivated this offer. In view of all other known expressions towards Reina from Beza and Olevianus this seems unlikely. My own reading of Olevianus's letter fails to sustain Böhmer in this regard, one of the very rare instances where I have not been in agreement with this fine and scrupulous scholar.

[33] This is referred to in the preceding note; with Olevianus signed Johannes Sylvanus and Franciscus Mosellanus; dated March 19, 1565.

[34] Which Reina repudiated vehemently at the onset of his March 24 letter to Strasbourg in response to Olevianus, et al. *BW* 2: p. 194.

[35] In which is included the administration of grace, incomprehensible to human reason. *Ibid.*, 2: p. 195. Cf. Ch. 1, section 4 of the 1559 Confession, fol. Av, in n. 21 above, and n. 22, for similar views on the mystery behind the sacraments, etc.

[36] It must be noted that a testimonial on Reina's behalf signed by 13 members of the Strasbourg church was appended to his March 24 letter; however, this and all signatures are in exactly the same handwriting as Reina's own correspondance. On the other hand that does not automatically invalidate the testimonial either. Rather, as I suggest below, it introduces a note of ambiguity into one's analysis of the situation.

[37] *BW*, 2: pp. 173, 177 ff, 192-211, 216-19; Tollin, 32: p. 247 ff; Van Lennep, p. 360 f n. 1; Lehnemann, pp. 91, 158 f.

[38] Reprinted in *BW*, 2: pp. 208-09.   See also the exchange between him and Beza, pp. 202-08.

[39] All the above-cited documents are replete with scriptural supports, in the texts and margins.   Possibly, too, the nod towards the Lutherans viz. the Eucharist reflected *already* their warmness towards him discussed below.

[40] *BW*, 2: pp. 173-74 n 32.

[41] Adolf Fluri, " Die Bärenbibel: Cassiodoro de Reinas Spanische Bibelübersetzung," *Gutenberg-Jahrbuch*, 9 nos. 2-3 (1923): pp. 3-23. My thanks go to Dr. Gustav Ungerer of Bern for bringing this important article, which utilized the Basel archives, to my notice, as well as providing me with a most helpful offprint of it.   For Valera's role here see the next chapter.   Cf. *BW*, 2: p. 173 ff.   Böhmer has reprinted one of Reina's letters regarding the Bible project in *Romanische Studien*, 4 (1880): pp. 485-86, which was dated September 27, 1567 from Strasbourg.   That does not, however, support without reservation Tollin's contention in 32: p. 247 that Reina resided at Strasbourg continuously from 1565-67, and all other data points towards the Frankfurt location for these years with the occasionally noted trips to Basel and Strasbourg.

[42] *BW*, 2: p. 177.   Fluri, whose main concern is how the book was produced is largely uninterested in Reina as an individual.   However, he did reprint two of Reina's letters on the subject, and included some useful illustrations from the original.   One of these (p. 5) suggests strongly Reina's reverence for Oeclampadius, the great Zwinglian reformer of Basel, although perhaps this was merely a courteous bow to the city fathers.

[43] And also of Johan Sturm, of whose benevolence towards Reina, see below, especially n. 45; *BW*, 2: p. 176.   Whether or not Reina worked on an edition of Bucer's works with Sturm, and some notable Lutherans such as the Marbach who was to lead Strasbourg completely to that faith in 1577 and who was a very violent anti-Calvinist, around 1565 I have not been able to verify.   Cf. Tollin, 31: p. 395 ff. and 32: p. 246 f.; *Polem.*: p. 73.

[44] Tollin, 31: p. 396 f; Lehnemann, p. 127.   One assumes that he taught the latter Spanish, and possibly Latin.   Perhaps the families were Sephardic originally.

[45] These letters are in *PSP*, 51: pp. 175-77 and *CSP*, Foreign. Elizabeth, 9: p. 124.

[46] Van Lennep, p. 360 f n. 1.

[47] *BW*, 2: pp. 216-21 for Reina's notes.   Generally see *Ibid.*, 2: p. 177. f; Van Lennep, p. 360 n. 1; Tollin, 32: p. 247 ff; Lehnemann, pp. 91, 158 f, all of which parallels his attacks on Corro.   In these three notices, two to Beza, and one to the Frankfurt congregation, Reina felt impelled to single out the moral accusations for especial repudiation, which

naturally meant they were once again being raised. Van Schelven, p. 324 f has particularly shown Beza's relentless hostility to the Spaniard at this time.

⁴⁸ Same as n. 47. Quite possibly his friendship with eminent Lutherans like Marbach, Sulzer, and Köchlein served him well in this regard.

⁴⁹ Van Schelven, p. 330 ff. He suggested Reina was an outright liar full of " haughty protestations."

⁵⁰ Cf. Lehnemann, p. 158f with *BW*, 2: p. 217.

⁵¹ Very brief discussions of these years are in *BW*, 2: p. 178; Lehnemann, p. 136 f; Van Schelven, p. 324 f; Tollin, 32: p. 247 ff. According to the last he made a brief trip to Strasbourg in 1570 to wind up the aforementioned Bucer collaborative edition with Sturm and Matthias Ritter, another eminent Lutheran, ever after a close friend and counsellor to Reina during his subsequent Antwerp ministry. Sulzer and Köchlein, now both at Strasbourg, housed him. It seems undeniable that the cordiality he continued to receive from these Lutherans prepared the ground for his conversion to that religion in 1578.

⁵² Van Schelven, p. 324 f, presumably a Calvinist post, although no one knows.

⁵³ This is discussed inconclusively in *ibid.*, p. 326 f; *BW*, 2: p. 178; Van Lennep, p. 368 ff; Schickler, 1: p. 232 ff, which last also contains the best account of the proceedings in London leading to his formal vindication.

⁵⁴ *CSP.*, Span., 2: p. 630.

⁵⁵ *Ibid.*, Span., 2: p. 653. See previous discussions of smuggling.

⁵⁶ E.g. Hauben, "A Spanish Calvinist Church."

⁵⁷ At the March 22 hearing with the French, not, as far as I know, before Grindal's panel. See Schickler, 1: p. 232ff. Note next chapter for Valera's seemingly consistent Calvinist orthodoxy, as against Reina and Corro. Presumably he and Reina had kept in touch over common biblical interests, although if this was so the correspondence failed to survive.

⁵⁸ Schickler, 1: p. 232, and n. 53 above.

⁵⁹ *Ibid.*, 1: p. 123 n.; Van Schelven, p. 326 f.

⁶⁰ Notes 44-45 above. For the subsequent printing of that Bible in England see Gustav Ungerer's illuminating article, " The Printing of Spanish Books in Elizabethan England," *The Library*, Fifth Ser., 20 no. 3 (1965): p. 183 ff.

⁶¹ Van Schelven, p. 327.

⁶² Schickler, 1: p. 232 ff.

[63] Reprinted in Lehnemann, pp. 160-62. My great thanks go to Dr. Benjamin Hill of the University of Illinois for translating the extremely difficult Latin. The following citations are taken from these pages.

[64] But cf. Reina's statement in this area made in 1593, discussed below.

[65] No evidence exists to suggest he preached to the Frankfurt Calvinists during 1571-78.

[66] Van Lennep, pp. 368 ff; *BW*, 2: p. 179 who ascribes the printing and circulation of these articles to some Antwerp Calvinists. Reina addressed himself to this point in 1593 to single out a Calvinist pastor named Willerius as the culprit (see below for the 1593 remarks). At this time Reina anticipated his much later observations by reaffirming his adherence to the Augsburg and Wittenberg Confessions. The latter, as Böhmer shrewdly saw, was mainly Bucer's endeavor which received occasional Calvinist praise, as late as from Guy de Brès in the 1560's. Melanchthon, of course, was to the Calvinists probably the least objectionable of the Lutheran leaders, although the Augsburg Confession in its day was considered more conciliatory to the Catholics than any other faith (Calvinism, naturally, hardly existed at the time of its composition). Lastly, but most emphatically not least, these 5 eucharistic articles, as far as they go, follow Bullinger's 1566 Second Helvetic Confession, to which Corro frequently pledged adherence. This important document may be conveniently consulted in *Reformed Confessions of the 16th Century*, A. C. Cochrane, ed. (Phila., 1966, paper ed.); pp. 220-301, especially pp. 277-88 on the sacraments and the Eucharist.

[67] For this situation see Pt. 1, ch. 2.

[68] Rahlenbeck, *L'Inq.*, p. 191. In 1593 Reina indicated his continuing dislike of Flaccius's party. Note Corro's bitter wrangling with him in Pt. 1, ch. 2.

[69] On one occasion they obtained his brief suspension. See Lehnemann pp. 90 ff, 101 ff; Van Lennep, p. 370 n. 1; *BW*, 2: p. 182; Rahlenbeck, *L'Inq.*, p. 191 ff. On occasion emissaries from Germany came to investigate local conditions, but Reina always obtained his way sustained by support from Ritter and other old friends. His complaints about the inability of Lutheranism to recruit native clergy are an interesting index of the faith's slide into apathy in the 1580's in the Low Countries. Obviously he believed, rightly I feel, that Netherlandish Lutheranism could not forever rely on imported Germans, ignorant of local conditions. Viz. Villiers can one call Reina a minor irenicist in Antwerp?

[70] With the exception of instances such as described in the preceding note.

[71] Recounted in Lehnemann, p. 111 et sqq. He remained there until his death nine years later.

106

[72] See *ibid.*, Appendices, which graphically demonstrate the Germanizing process over many years; also *BW*, 2: p. 184.

[73] Van Lennep, p. 371; Van Schelven, p. 325. His son, Marcus Cassiodoro, followed him in the Lutheran ministry; another, Agostino Cassiodoro, became a translator and tutor in several languages. See *BW*, 2: pp. 185 ff on them.

[74] Reprinted in Lehnemann, pp. 162-69; again I record my gratitude to Dr. Hill.

[75] Cf. notes 64 and 66 above; he roundly denied having done the trilingual version of the London " Swiss " articles.

II. CYPRIANO DE VALERA (c. 1532 - 16??)

Our knowledge of Cypriano de Valera exists almost in directly
inverse proportion to his importance. Like Corro and Reina
his conversion to Calvinism occurred during his youthful days
at San Isidro. In addition to several original tracts,[1] Valera
produced the definitive Castilian Bible in 1602, working from
previously described ones, chiefly Reina's. His remained for
centuries the standard basis for evangelizing Protestant missionaries in the Hispanic world.[2] That achievement alone stamps
him as a personage of some singificance; yet our ignorance of
much of Valera's career extends even to confusion as to where
and when he died.[3] Singularly, however, there is no indication
that he departed from the straight path of Calvinism, very much
unlike his monkish compatriots.[4]

McFadden includes Valera with those who slipped out of
Spain in 1557, but others think he may have fled as early as
1552.[5] Whatever the year he did go immediately to Geneva, too,
in typical San Isidrian fashion. But it was not until October 10,
1558 that his stay there can be certified, as it were, when, with
eight other Spaniards he took the *habitant's* civic eath.[6] Probably
the most important results of his indeterminable sojourn there
were the beginnings of his biblical work and the continuation of
close relationships with his fellow former monks.[7]

The passing of Mary Tudor drew Valera, with so many other
Protestant emigres, to Elizabeth's England. It does not appear
that he obtained the kind of highly placed English connections
which characterized, varyingly, the other subjects of this study,
but nonetheless " by special grace in 1559 " Valera was awarded

is possible to know more this interpretation must skirt about the matter of his presumed relations with Reina, however. Backed by the new Italian pastor, Aureli, Valera carried the day against the Farías faction, not without considerable stress on all concerned. Not until March, 1572 was the affair concluded, during which period Farías and others had been barred from communion; ultimately all were reconciled to the congregation.

That, however, did not mean Valera replaced Corro as the informal pastor to the Spanish " conventicle " within this church. Evidence either way is spare to the extreme. Hutton has categorically called Valera " pastor of the Spanish congregation." Since he failed to give a date, much less indicate whether he meant something like Reina's independent Spanish Church of 1559-65 or Corro's " conventicles " within the French and Italian ones respectively, such a statement is virtually meaningless, not to mention confusing. It is true that in a 1583 report to the Privy Council on foreigners living in London Valera was listed as a " preacher," [20] but it is impossible to clarify what that title meant since no congregational designation was attached to it. Quite plausibly one may infer that in view of Valera's two English degrees in divinity this was a courtesy title, much as the holder of a PhD. today is often called Doctor. Whatever the case it also might have reflected his greatly improved financial situation. This resulted from two unrelated factors. In the will of his old compatriot, Baptista, dated July 14, 1573, Valera was named one of several beneficiaries.[21] Presumably the Genevese was childless, and that Valera alone of the remaining San Isidrians was one of his heirs testified probably to a long-maintained friendship. Secondly, his eldest son, who used the name John Cyprian de Cardenas (according to his naturalization of April 11, 1583), had become one of Walsingham's trusted agents and secretaries.[22] Since at one point the younger Valera had been jointly commended by the Queen, Burghley, and Sir Robert Cecil, it seems safe to assume that the father benefited from his son's success. The apparent calm of Valera's life after the minor imbroglio with Farías in 1571-72 probably was in some considerable part due to this, as well as to Baptista's munificence.

He interrupted his writing labors to preach heresy to captured Spanish sailors at Bridewell jail in the Armada's aftermath;[23] otherwise he had become strictly a scholar, Apparently because he obtained more favorable conditions for publishing the Bible he moved to Holland in 1599 or 1600. He was able to enlist the support of leading Remonstrants like Arminius and Uytenbogaert to help smooth over a misunderstanding with his publisher; in fact he boarded with Uytenbogaert in Amsterdam. Yet in November, 1602 he applied personally to Maurice of Nassau at Leiden for aid apparently concerning the Bible.[24] With that he dropped permanently from sight.

It is tantalizing to think of Valera in theological accord with the Arminians late in life. While, however, it is clear that the latter, both in England and the Netherlands, looked favorably on the deceased Corro, nothing links Valera doctrinally to them. On the basis of presently known data we can only assume that Valera's connection with the Remonstrant doctors was purely personal. It might be helpful, too, to note that during the first few years of the seventeenth century the breach between the Arminians and the Gomarists was yet to take the ferociously orthodox form it achieved at Dort nearly two decades later. Rather, it makes some sense, at least, to envision Valera disagreeing with his Remonstrant friends without that envenoming their cordial relationship. This detail, obviously, runs counter to the argument in the rest of the study, but I believe it fits the available facts; and not all were Bezas, Cousins, and Corros. Certainly all concerned here would have sharted a warm desire to see Valera's Castilian Bible in print and en route, clandestinely of course, to Spain.[25]

---

[1] The original of these are reprinted in *RAE*, 6. They are characterized by a notably virulent anti-papal tone. The British Museum, the Newberry Library, and other major research centers possess varying editions and translations of all Valera's works.

[2] Linnhoff, p. 42. Probably one should say the Reina-Valera Bible.

[3] Fluri, p. 20, says he died in England shortly after the printing of the 1602 Bible; the other two commonly assumed years of his demise are 1622 and 1625. E.g. the catalogs of Harvard and Yale University libraries give '25. *BW*, 3: pp. 147-75 studies Valera, but only ten pp. are narrative; the rest are bibliographical. Lewis J. Hutton, " The Spanish Heretic: Cypriano de Valera," *Church History*, 27 (March, 1958): pp. 23-31 is a poor and confusing brief summary which I attack in a forthcoming short notice in *Hispania Sacra*. I have incorporated the latter here. The English genealogical work in 1900 by N. V. Fenn, *Cypriano de Valera and his Descendants* is extremely difficult to obtain, and I have never seen it. As far as I know only the British Museum had a copy which has been mislaid, permanently unfortunately.

[4] Note, however, the connection he had as an old man with the Dutch Arminians, discussed below.

[5] McFadden, p. 54; *RAE*, 1: pp. x-xi.

[6] Paul Geisendorf, *Livre des Habitants de Genève* (Geneva, 1957): 1: p. 137 f.

[7] E.g. Linnhoff, p. 42 and J. B. G. Galiffe, *Le Refuge italien de Genève* (Geneva, 1881): p. 169 which suggest the bloc nature of the handful of Spaniards who grouped themselves in the Italian Church at Geneva after the end of a short-lived Spanish congregation headed respectively by Juan Pérez and Reina. In this regard directly concerning Valera see n. 21 below. Fluri, p. 19, says Valera " stopped in Geneva for some time." In his M. S. Top. Oxon. c. 12: p. 169 Wiffen indicated his belief that Valera had assisted Reina in composing the controversial 1559 Confession of Faith for the London Spanish. Since Valera testified on Reina's behalf in the " rehabilitation " proceedings of 1578-79, all discussed in the last chapter, Wiffen may well be right, although I know of no corroborative evidence. Cf. n. 11 in the Reina ch. I owe this reference to Dr. Ungerer of Bern, again. The point here is that any such collaboration, as well as the specific matter described in n. 21 would be derived from the common San Isdrian background as maintained in Geneva, and occasionally, beyond.

[8] I owe this information to Dr. Edward M. Wilson, and through him his colleague, Dr. Bruce Dickins. The references are J. and J. A. Venn, *Alumni Cantabrigiensis* (Cambridge, 1927): 1: p. iv; John Venn, *Grace Book* (Cambridge, 1910): p. 140 ff; E. K. Purnell, *University of Cambridge, College Histories: Magdalene College* (London, 1904). Not only were Cambridge fellows not permitted to marry at this time, but for long afterwards according to Dr. Wilson who kindly supplied me with this pertinent domestic information. As we have been with Corro Cambridge generally seems to have been more rigorous than Oxford in this period ! Fluri, p. 19, dates Valera's start at Oxford in 1556, which clearly must have been a printer's error. Linnhoff, p. 39, and

113

Van Lennep, p. 374 f n. 2 also have slightly erroneous chronology concerning Valera at Cambridge.

[9] This thesis is convincingly prepounded more broadly by Wm. M. Jones, " Foreign Teachers in Sixteenth Century England," *The Historian*, 21 (1958-59): pp. 162-75.

[10] See n. 8 above; Ungerer discussed throughout his book and article cited above the growing interest in things Spanish as Elizabeth's reign progressed.

[11] P.R.O.: S. P. 46/24 fol 236. This mss. also contains a short testimonial on behalf of Valera and a German student by William Goldingham, fellow of Trinity Hall, late of Magdalene, noting the two are members of the latter college by the " Queen's gift." It is also undated and unaddressed. Dr. Ungerer brought my notice to it.

[12] E.g. the future Bishop Walsh according to Van Lennep, p. 374 f n. 2 and Linnhoff, p. 39.

[13] Alexander Grosart, *The Townley Hall MSS* (Privately printed, 1877): p. 100. Nowell's brother was Dean Alexander Nowell. I owe this reference to Dr. Patrick Collinson of King's College, London.

[14] *HSP*, 10: pp. i, 441 and 10: pp. ii, 192 for 1568 and 1571 respectively.

[15] Firpo, p. 364.

[16] See n. 7 above for Valera's relations with his fellow former monks.

[17] See Pt. 1, ch. 3, n. 67 above. Farías had become a small-scale artisan in London who had been naturalized as early as February 27, 1562. Ironically, some years later he left the Italian Church to rejoin the French which he had belonged to around 1564 (obviously after Reina's exodus). Scattered bits of information about him can be consulted in *HSP*, 8, 10: pp. i-ii, and 38, and in the Swiss works by Galiffe and Geisendorf previously cited.

[18] Firpo, p. 364. What follows on this episode is from Firpo, pp. 364-71. It seems appropriate to note here that as this conflict appears to have stemmed from purely personal grounds (although I suggest other possibilities below) its character fits well within the general framework of the study.

[19] Hutton, p. 27. Ungerer, " Printing ": p. 216 said " it seemed, however, that... Valera was appointed minister in succession to Corro [after the latter's suspension in Mar., 1569]. This caused a violent rupture between the two..." Despite my high regard for Dr. Ungerer's fine scholarship I must evaluate this as needing more definite proof, although if so it accounts for n. 20, probably.

[20] *HSP*, 10: pp. ii, 315. See also 10: pp. i, 441 and pp. ii, 192 for further information.

[21] Baptista was one of the few San Isidrians who settled permanently in Geneva, where he became a successful merchant. Linnhoff, p. 42, mistakenly list him as a merchant from Seville, but cf. McFadden, p. 54.

[22] Cardenas' career is recounted in Ungerer, *Anglo-Spanish*...: p. 93 f; see also *HSP*, 8: p. 65 and *CSP*, Foreign. Elizabeth (1590): p. 648.

[23] Recounted in Strype, *Annals*, 3: pp. ii, 23 who noted that it was Valera's plea during one of these visits on behalf of a Giles Corit, a Breton claiming to have been impressed into the Spanish navy, that obtained him freedom.

[24] Linnhoff, p. 42; Van Lennep, p. 390; Böhmer, " Prot. Prop.": p. 385 f; Wiffen, M. S. Top. Oxon. c. 12: p. 169.

[25] The story of such smuggling has been treated by Böhmer, " Prot. Prop.": and more recently in my previously cited *Historical Journal* article. McFadden returns to the topic often throughout his thesis; cf. our Pt. I.

APPENDIX: ADRIAN SARAVIA
(c. 1530 - 1613)

When one considers that Adrian Saravia was not only born outside of and never visited Spain, was as frequently called a Dutchman as often as a Spaniard then and later, and appears to have had no communications with persons like Corro during times when all lived nearby and intermingled with the same groups, perhaps one may justifiably question his inclusion in this study. Indeed, his sole claim to being Spanish, which he himself seems not to have done, lay in that his father was. The latter, however, had emigrated to Artois, where he wed a native wife. Adrian, one of several children, came into the world around 1530 in the town of Hesdin.[1] Like Corro he was to move from Catholicism to Calvinism to Anglicanism, albeit in very differing ways. Saravia was Gui de Brès's junior collaborator in the composition of the first Netherlandish Reformed Confession of Faith, printed in 1563; more significantly, from 1607 he was one of the translators for the King James Bible. Along the way he was Rector of the University of Leiden and subsequently, a major controversialist against the presbyterian forms of church government and discipline, which earlier he had done much to implement, and a vigorous proponent of what shortly evolved into High Church Episcopacy. Such details strongly suggest that at least a passing notice of him is in order, especially considering that not even a brief study of recent vintage exists.[2] His father's nationality serves as the technical *point d'appui*.

Presumably sometime in the mid-1550's Saravia accepted Calvinism for by 1557 he had fled his Franciscan monastery at St. Omer.[3] From this point on materials about him are available

116

in nearly directly inverse proportion to his importance. Probably in 1559 he arrived in England. Nothing extant supports several assertions that he studied briefly at Oxford.[4] After an initial, friendly association with Nicholas des Gallars, then minister of the London French Church, he joined the capitol's Dutch congregation.[5] Obviously Saravia laid the foundations for his superb abilities in English during this first two-year sojourn in London. Less obviously, perhaps, inasmuch as even those like Strype who certainly were knowledgable about men like Corro and Saravia failed to see it, it seems inconceivable that Saravia, in the course of his involvement with these two Strangers' Churches, would not have been aware of Reina's fledgling Spanish Church in London, not to mention Reina's early theological difficulties with the French. While I believe I am right to think he almost surely knew Reina, and quite probably other Spanish refugees, the proof is regrettably absent.

Sometime in late 1561 or early 1562 in response to a call from Antwerp for his services Saravia returned to the continent; shortly thereafter he helped found the Walloon Church in Brussels with the ill-fated Jean de Marnix.[6] Around this time he began to collaborate with De Brès and several others on the Confession. By this brief time Saravia was already well up the socio-ecclesiastical ladder in the Low Countries; he was among several selected to make the Confession's formal presentation to Orange and Egmont, while his brother-in-law performed a similar ceremony with Louis of Nassau.[7] However, this triumph was somewhat cut short; Philip II's pressure on the seventeen provinces for religious and administrative conformity led among other things to Saravia's reembarkation for England, and ultimately De Brès's execution, in 1563 and 1567 respectively.

But for some very brief trips back to the Low Countries Saravia spent much the better part of the years 1563-78 in the British Isles, as headmaster of Elizabeth College on Guersney in the Channel Islands, pastor of the Walloon Church at Southampton, and one of the ministers to the London Dutch Church, in that order. The details of his functions at these places are not our concern, falling as they do chiefly in the realm of ministerial

117

and pedagogical routine.[8] What is significant, however, is that personages like William Cecil were instrumental in obtaining for Saravia some of his English posts, and generally many of the men figuring in the previous accounts of Corro, Reina, and Valera, reappear in broadly similar roles here.[9] Furthermore, during so substantial if occasionally interrupted a residence in London, Saravia must have learned of Corro's doings, given their protracted and well-publicized nature, even if relevant documentary data are unavailable for proof. That they moved in often identical circles strengthens this hypothesis. Almost certainly Saravia supported the orthodox Calvinists, although ironically circumstances after 1587 were to confront him with some of Corro's bitterest enemies, who now similarly reviled him.

By the early 1580's, then, Adrian Saravia doubtless deserved his eminence as a " prudent, sincere, and moderate " Calvinist divine.[10] His fall from Calvinist grace, as it were, commenced shortly after this accolade.

Parma's relentless military pressure drove Saravia along with hundreds of other Calvinist ministers and laymen from Ghent to Tournai to Antwerp to Leiden in the early and mid-1580's.[11] His career at the famed University of Leiden was meteoric: in less than five years he had moved to its Rectorship, although as Meyerhoff has shown, he kept up contacts with his old Guersney community.[12] At Leiden he pursued two courses which soon proved difficult to maintain simultaneously: on the one hand the staunch advocate of orthodoxy against persons such as Koolhaes and Coornhert; on the other, from at least 1584, an important figure in the conspiracy to make the Earl of Leicester permanent Governor-General of the Netherlands.[13] Maurice of Nassau's decisive *contre-coup* nipped well in advance any possibility of success for the Leicester faction, and Saravia was excluded from the subsequent amnesty, which testified to his significant role in the plot.[14] By this time, however, he was safe in England, from where he issued a series of letters to former friends like Villiers and Arnoldus and to the Provincial Council of Holland in vain attempts to obtain a new ruling in his favor.[15] This failure led directly to Saravia's theological *volte-face*; also from this time he was awarded a series of Anglican livings, culminating in the prebendary of Canterbury. He fell short, however, of becoming a bishop, his great aim during these years.[16] In this final Anglican phase, Saravia's friends and acquaintances ranged from Richard Hooker (cf. the Corro chapters) to Isaac Causabon.[17]

Saravia's primary historical significance, aside from his enduring contributions to the 1611 Bible, resulted from his energetic polemics defending episcopacy, begun in 1590, which as Dr. Thompson of King's College, Cambridge, has recently shown, greatly influenced the new anti-presbyterian (and in the English sense of the term, Arminian) generation.[18] Again it seems highly improbable that he did not know Corro, or at least his writings by this stage, although such observations must remain at the level of plausible speculation.

The 1591 *Collection of Sermons and Writings*,[19] published in London, is a convenient point of departure, which sustains Dr. Thompson's analysis of Saravia's *De Diversis Ministrorum Evangelii Gradibus* of 1590. One observes with interest that the *Collection* was dedicated respectively to Archbishop Whitgift, Lord Burghley (the former William Cecil), and Sir Christopher Hatton, one of the Queen's most favored courtiers. Hatton is credited with housing Saravia on his arrival from Holland in 1587, while Burghley had expedited the transformation of the exile's previously-granted denizen status into full naturalized citizenship; Whitgift, not surprisingly, appears to have been the chief agent in Saravia's acceptance of Anglicanism and rapid settling into what was called here " a fair pastoral province."

The dedication was followed by an " Epistle to the Ministers of the Low Countries " in which Saravia recalled his lamentations at Leiden over " the state of the Church there." Whether this belated recrimination was true is impossible to say. We have only political evidence concerning Saravia's rude break with Calvinism and flight from Holland. From this he went on to blame all the Church's difficulties in the Netherlands on its non-episcopalian structure. Among other things he attacked ministerial poverty there, which presumably compared poorly with the greater comfort of the English clergy; oddly, he suggested that only the death of William of Orange and Leicester had precluded the superior form of church government from succeeding across the Channel. His naiveté in this area, if we may call it that, was summed up in his charge that secular " magistrates " had usurped Catholic lands and revenues which should have gone directly for the churches' maintenance; he omits Henry VIII's reign in this regard. The remainder of these tracts more or less repeat in varying form, with customary dense scriptural quoting, Saravia's new-found faith in episcopalian virtues. As Thompson demonstrates, he came to consider the institution of bishops not merely apostolic, but founded by Christ himself.[20] The *Collection* and Saravia's other apologetics soon aroused the aged Beza's ire; typically, he called the apostate a " petulant insulter." [21] Thrusting aside initial hesitations about entering this fray publicly, he engaged Saravia (and others) in a running series of sharp polemics in the 1590's.[22]

Saravia subsequently anticipated the political aspects of church-state relations in his " Letter to the Ministers of the Isle of Guernsey." [23] In view of the fact that some three decades earlier he had been instrumental in the Elizabethan but Reformed ecclesiastical organization there this appeal to the Guernsey divines to recognize the superiority of their King and his Bishop of Winchester, while he derided their present " French " discipline, rang ironically. He commented further that " the Parliament's authority is great, but without the King's assent [to its decrees] nothing takes the rigor of law." Saravia continued his previously-printed tirades against Beza, the French, the Scotch, et al, throughout this piece, accompanied by a renewed affirmation of the necessity of episcopal ordination for all lesser clergy. Demonstrating his knowledge of peculiarly local traditions he brushed aside the Guernsey clergy's claims to special privileges derived from Norman centuries. In concluding he burst out bitterly against Calvinism in general once more: " Were your Discipline armed with power as the Inquisition of *Spain* (original italics) is, it would surpass it in tyranny. The Episcopal authority is canonical... the Bishop is but the Keeper of the Laws... and [he is empowered thereby] to punish the transgressors of your Consistories and Synods." I might add that I believe it quite plausible that Saravia meant the " transgressions " as well as the " transgressors " in this last point.

Saravia's dissertation on the Eucharist, dedicated to James I, was reprinted in 1855, and contrains a very helpful biographical sketch.[24] It is interesting to compare his treatment of so thorny and vital a question with what Corro and Reina had to say on the subject. In the Preface to the Reader he touches the familiar irenic cord: " Satan, the sower of the tares of discord, hath brought it to pass that the Sacrament of peace and innermost union... hath become the watchword of a deadly and exterminating war, with [comparatively little] hope... of reconciliation." [25] He moves on to say that he does not wish to upset previous concords, such as those concluded much earlier in Germany at Augsburg, Wittenberg, etc., for he believed it yet possible " to blot out all dissension touching the Sacrament and to unite... the Churches of Christ," which sentiment squarely contradicts the one just cited.[26]

Saravia then definies the Eucharist in terms which probably failed to add clarity to this already muddled aspect and the age's penchant for abstruse theological controversy.[27] After what is to this reader a rather baffling account of the dispute he claimed that " Christ in His Supper did in truth and reality deliver to his disciples His Body and His Blood, the manner [of which] is beyond human understanding and must be left to God." A bit later, possibly troubled by his own vagueness to that point, Saravia added that the Eucharist consists of " the outward visible sign of the invisible heavenly thing united sacramentally to the sign." [28] A lengthy scriptural narrative of relevant matters followed, stressing Irenaeus and Augustine, and towards the work's end, Saravia attempted to use Bucer to link the Anglican with the Swiss positions (Zwingli and Oeclampadius, *not* Calvin and Beza) in this matter.[29]

Pretty clearly Saravia did not consider himself a Spaniard,[30] as Corro in particular did, and as Reina and Valera most certainly were. Nonetheless, he warrants a small niche in this study of several Spanish Reformation heretics. Excepting Valera, he resembles them in his revolt against Catholicism and then within Protestantism, and like them all he had the useful knack of obtaining the patronage of the great wherever he went. Singularly, however, his withdrawl from Calvinism (or more fairly, at least initially, its repudiation of him) stemmed from apparently completely secular grounds, some *ex post facto* remarks from Saravia notwithstanding. Obviously a man of considerable ability and energy, Saravia's record, incompletely known no doubt, suggest he was an important figure of the second rank among Reformation personages. I would hope that even more so concerning him than the other three studied here, this brief notice will stimulate the merited and comprehensive research which his stature demands, and which contemporaries seemed well aware of.[31]

---

[1] On this general background see brief notices in Strype, *Annals*, 1: p. 224; A. A. Van Schelven, *Kerkeraads-Protocollen der Nederduitsche Vluchtelingen-Kerk te Londen, 1560-63* (Amsterdam, 1921): p. 395 n. 2 (hereafter cited as *K-P*); Jean Meyerhoff, " Adrien Saravia," *Bulletin de la Société d'Histoire du Protestantisme belge* Ser. 2 (July, 1921): p. 68; G. F. Hodges and W. Rolleston, " Adrian Saravia, First Headmaster of Elizabeth College," *Société Guernesiaise: Reports and Transactions* 12 (1933): p. 57. On some minor details, such as the parents, these are not always identical, while the Hodges-Rolleston notice seems unevenly documented. Meyerhoff has a useful bibliographical note, p. 74 n.

[2] Note the dates of the citations above. Brief attention is given Saravia in connection with certain disputes and polemics in England in the 1590's in H. C. Porter, *op. cit.*, ch. 15 and W. Cargill Thompson, " Anthony Marten and the Elizabethan Debate on Episcopacy," in *Essays in Modern English Church History in memory of Norman Sykes*, G. V. Bennett & J. D. Walsh, editors (Oxford University Press, 1966): pp. 57-62, 71, 73 f. On p. 352 f Porter calls him a Dutchman. Thompson is aware of Saravia's significance, but of necessity cannot take a fuller view of his varied and impressive career.

³ J. W. de Grave, " Notes on the Register of the Walloon Church of Southampton and on the Churches of the Channel Islands," *Proceedings of the Huguenot Society of London* 5 (1894-96): p. 136 f; Schickler, *op. cit.*, 2: p. 372 and note; cf note 1.

⁴ E.g. Meyerhoff, p. 69; K. F. Prims, *Geschiedenis van Antwerpen* (Antwerp, 1938-43) 8 i: p. 51; and note 3.

⁵ Meyerhoff, p. 69; *HSP* 10 i: p. 278; Hodges, p. 57 f who quotes Des Gallars's letter to Calvin commending him.

⁶ Meyerhoff, p. 69; Prims 8 i: p. 51; *K-P*, 395 n. 2. Van Schelven also noted that Saravia often used the pseudonym Moravius (his numerous other ones are listed in Meyerhoff, p. 68 n. 1). A Moravius, was connected with the controversy about the heterodox friend of Reina's, Acontius, discussed earlier. Assuming this was Saravia, and recalling his relationship with Des Gallars, just noted above, he must have known Reina. See pp. 201 n. 1, 202, 229 and note 1.

⁷ Hodges, p. 58 f who calls the brothers-in-law a ' *valet de chambre* '; Meyerhoff, p. 69; Prims 8 i: p. 51 calls the brother-in-law a private chaplain to Louis.

⁸ Note 3 above; Meyerhoff and Hodges, *passim*. As late as 1584, however, he put in a brief tour as minister to the Southampton Walloon Church; see De Grave, p. 136 f. Hessls 3 i abounds with letters showing how much his services were in demand in the Low Countries, especially in 1577-78.

⁹ E.g. the letters reprinted in Hodges, pp. 64 ff; cf. Strype, *Annals* 1: pp. 223 ff.

¹⁰ Quoted in *Werken der Marnix-Vereeniging* (Utrecht, 1870-79) Ser. 3 v. 4: p. 37 (hereafter cited as *WMV*).

¹¹ Hodges, p. 70 f; Meyerhoff, p. 71 f; *WMV* 3 v. 1: p. 133, v. 3: p. 59.

¹² Meyerhoff, p. 72, which certainly suggest he was keeping all options open. Even if this was unconnected with the Leicester affair, it speaks volumes for the insecurity among the Calvinist clergy in areas such as the embattled Netherlands well into the century. Cf. De Grave, p. 147.

¹³ *Ibid.*, p. 73 and Hodges, p. 71 briefly summarize Saravia in this matter. See P. J. Blok, *History of the People of the Netherlands*, R. Putnam, transl. (New York, 1899-1900) 3: pp. 191, 196; Strype, *Annals* 3 i: p. 418, 3 ii: pp. 351 ff; Hodges, p. 71 for Saravia's appeal to Lord Burghley on June 9, 1585 calling for English aid and leadership in the Low Countries. See Hessels 2: pp. 719 et sqq. for several Saravia letters to Leicester's physician, Dr. James, during 1586 for similar sentiments.

¹⁴ Hodges, p. 71; Meyerhoff, p. 73; *WMV* Ser. 3 v. 3: p. 53. He was perpetually banished. According to *WMV* Ser. 2 v. 3: p. 565 he had

signed a petition in the fall of 1586 requesting that the Earl be made the University's formal patron in order to check its grave moral and theological deficiencies; obviously this was to be a screen for the Leicester faction's operations on his behalf.

[15] Reprinted in *WMV* Ser. 3 v. 5: pp. 299 ff, 362 ff and 3: p. 53 with replies from Villiers and Arnoldus. Justus Lipsius succeeded to the Rectorship at Leiden.

[16] Hodges, p. 71 f outlines his succession of posts from 1588; cf. De Grave, p. 137 and *HSP*, 15: p. 37.

[17] The lengthy introduction in *Saravia on the Eucharist*, Geo. A. Denison, tranl. (from the Latin; London, 1855) is very useful in this regard (hereafter cited as Denison). Denison relied heavily on Walton's famed biography of Hooker, from which one sees that Saravia was perhaps Hooker's closest friend from 1595-1600. Denison also included some excerpts from Saravia's pro-episcopal writings and some correspondence from Causabon to him. The British Museum has a copy.

[18] Thompson's relevant pp. are in note 2 above. On p. 57 he states that Saravia had left Holland because of England's " more congenial religious climate " than the former land's " dour Calvinism " offered; since he seems unaware of the central role of Saravia's political failure here this is misleading and out of context.

[19] I read this work on microfilm at Princeton University.

[20] Thompson, p. 57 and *et. sqq.* In one of the prefaces, " To the Reader," Saravia noted that Roman Catholic usage of bishops should not prejudice Englishmen against Anglicanism's use of them. Clearly he anticipated this kind of typical objection to episcopacy.

[21] Paul Geisendorf, *Bèze*, p. 385 f cites it. Strype, *Whitgift* 2: pp. 158 *et. sqq.* details Whitgift's support of Saravia, Sutcliffe, et al against Beza to the extent of reprimanding the latter for his use of personally abusive language in such matters. In these pp. he also shows the building up of English resentment since at least 1566 against Beza for his meddling in the internal ecclesiastical affairs of the country. Cf. Thompson, *passim*. Porter, *op. cit.*, ch. 15 and Strype, *ibid.*, 2: pp. 229 ff do show, however, that on the complicated William Barret case at Cambridge in 1595 Whitgift and Saravia did not quite agree. Barret had violently attacked the Puritan party on the predestination issue; the differences between the Archbishop and Saravia appear to have been over language and tactics rather than fundamentals. Barret ultimately recanted without losing his university offices, however. For more on Beza's attitude see his letter of August 27, 1595 to two London French pastors in Hessels 3 i: p. 871.

[22] Same as note 21.

[23] Reprinted in *Clavi Trabales*, N. Bernard, editor (London, 1661), part 5. Not surprisingly this collection supported episcopacy and royal supremacy. It is in the British Museum.

[24] See note 17 above.

[25] Denison, p. 13

[26] *Ibid.*, p. 17.

[27] *Ibid.*, pp. 17 ff.

[28] *Ibid.*, p. 23 f.

[29] *Ibid.*, pp. 119 ff, 143.

[30] On the other hand a Christofle de Saravia, who appears to have been one of his brothers, was admitted with his family to the aforementioned Southampton Church on July 3, 1569, and was buried there on November 20, 1572. He was classified as " *Espaignol de Nation.*" See De Grave, p. 136 f. Another article in this series with reference to Adrian Saravia is J. C. Moens, " Discipline of the French Church of London, 1578," 2: p. 46 where he is named as a minister to this church in that year. This detail, in turn, lends further support to my running remarks about his probable knowledge of Corro, et al. Also, see Guillaume Bogaert's letter from Ghent to the London Dutch Church on March 7, 1578 juxtaposing in the very same paragraph Corro unfavorably and Saravia laudatorily; in Hessels 3 i p. 501.

[31] Saravia is merely one of quite a few similarly significant but little known such figures. Mr. N. R. N. Tyacke of University College, London, informs me of the overriding importance for this same period of the Danish follower of Melanchthon, Nicholas Hemminges, who is mentioned favorably by Corro in one of his works. Neither Mr. Tyacke nor I are aware of any recent sholarship on Hemminges in one of the historians' major tongues. The Dane was one of the leading proponents of Protestant irenicism before 1600.

SOURCES

MANUSCRIPTS

1. BELGIUM

   Brussels. Archives générales du Royaume. Fonds: Papiers d'Etat et d'Audience.

2. ENGLAND

   Oxford. Univ. Oxon. Arch.: KK 9.
   Public Record Office: State Papers 46/24 fol 236.

3. FRANCE

   Archives départementales des Basses-Pyrénées: B 13.
   Bordeaux. Archives historiques du Département de la Gironde: 17.
   Paris. Bibliothèque Nationale: 43077 Ms Dupuy 103.
   Toulouse. Archives municipales: BB 11 Deliberations.

4. GERMANY

   Halle. Landesbibliothek, Universitäts Sachsen-Anhalt: Confession de Fe Christiana de Cassiodoro de Reina (1601 Spanish-German version by E. v. Retrodt at Cassel).

5. ITALY

   Turin. Archivio di Stato: folio 17.

6. SWITZERLAND

   Geneva. Musée historique de la Réformation: Corr. Eccl. Mss. fr. 407 v. 7.

CORRO'S WORKS
(IN CHRONOLOGICAL ORDER)

1. Letter to Cassiodoro de Reina, December 24, 1563 (The Theobon letter).

2. *Letter to the Lutheran Ministers of the Flemish Church of Antwerp*, January 2, 1567 (Antwerp).

3. *Letter to Philip II*, March 15, 1567 (Antwerp).

4. *Tableau de l'Œuvre de Dieu*, July 15, 1569 (Norwich).

5. *A Theological Dialogue*, 1575 (London).

6. *Paraphrase and Commentary on Ecclesiastes*, May 16, 1579 (London).

PRINTED COLLECTIONS

Antwerpsch Archievenblad. 1864-1932. Ser. 1 v. II (Antwerp).

Beza, Theodore. 1573-1575. *Epistolarum Theologicarum* (2 v., Geneva).

Böhmer, Eduard. 1874-1904. *Bibliotheca Wiffeniana* (3 v., London-Strasbourg).

Calendar of State Papers.

Cochrane, A. C., editor. 1966. *Reformed Confessions of the 16th Century* (Philadelphia).

Corpus Reformatorum. v 45-48.

Crespin, Jean, 1885. *Histoire des Martyrs* (vl., Toulouse).

Hessels, J. H. 1889-1897. *Ecclesiae londine-batavae Archivum* (3 v. in 4, Cambridge).

Parker Society Publications.

Poullet, Edmond and Piot, Charles. 1877-1896. *Correspondance du Cardinal Granvelle* (12 v., Brussels).

Publications of the Huguenot Society of London. 1893-1937 (v 8, 10, 37, London).

Usez y Rio, Luis. 1847-1880. *Reformistas antiguos españoles* (22 v, Madrid-London).

Van den Brink, Backhuizen, Theissen, J. S., and Van Gelder, Enno. 1925-1942. *Correspondance de Marguerite de Parme avec Philippe II* (3 v, Utrecht).

McNeill, J. T., editor, 1957. *Calvin: On the Christian Faith* (New York-Indianapolis).

PERIODICALS AND SECONDARY WORKS

Böhmer, Eduard. 1901. "Antonio del Corro," *BSHPF* 50: pp. 201-216.

— 1880. " Ein Brief von Cassiodoro de Reyna," *Romanische Stüdien*: 4 pp. 483-486.

— 1897. " Protestantische Propaganda in Spanien im Anfänge des 17 Jahrhunderts," *Zeitschrift für Kirchengeschichte* 17: pp. 373-390.

Boer, C. 1952. *Hofpredigers van Prins Willem van Oranje* (S'Gravanhague).

Curtis, Mark. 1959. *Oxford and Cambridge in Transition, 1558-1642* (Oxford).

Devic, Cl. and Vaisette, J. 1889. *Histoire générale de Languedoc* (v 11, Toulouse).

Firpo, Luigi. 1951. " Francesco Pucci in Inghilatera," *Revue internationale de Philosophie* 5: pp. 158-173.

— 1959. " La chiesa italiana di Londra nel Cinquecento e i suoi rapporti con Ginevra," in *Ginevra e L'Italia* (Florence): pp. 307-412.

Fluri, Adolf. 1923. " Die Bärenbibel: Cassiodoro de Reinas Spanische Bibelübersetzung," *Gutenberg-Jahrbuch* 9 nos. ii-iii: pp. 3-23.

Fruin, R. 1900. " Het Voorspel van den Tachtigjarigen Oolog." in his *Verspreide Geschriften* (S'Gravenhague) 1: pp.246-449.

Galiffe, J. 1881. *Le refuge italien de Genève* (Geneva).

Geisendorf, Paul. 1957. *Le livre des Habitants de Genève* (v 1, Geneva).

— 1949. *Theodore de Bèze* (Geneva).

Grosart, Alexander. 1877. *The Townley Hall MSS* (London ?).

Hauben, Paul J. 1965. "A Spanish Calvinist Church in Elizabethan London, 1559-1565," *Church History* 34: pp. 50-56.

— 1966. " In Pursuit of Heresy: Spanish Diplomats vs. Spanish Heretics in France and England during the Wars of Religion," *Historical Journal* 9 iii: pp. 275-285.

— 1967. " Marcus Pérez and Marrano Calvinism in the Dutch Revolt and the Reformation," *Bibliothèque d'Humanisme et Renaissance* 29: pp. 121-132.

— 1967. " Reform and Counterreform: The Case of the Spanish Heretics " in a memorial vol. of essays as yet untitled in honor of E. H. Harbison (Princeton).

— 1967 (?). "A Note on the Spanish Heretic: Cypriano de Valera," *Hispania Sacra* 18 fasc. 1 in Spanish.

Hutton, L. J. 1958. " The Spanish Heretic: Cypriano de Valera," *Church History* 27: pp. 23-31.

Jacquot, Jean. 1953. " Sébastien Castellion et l'Angleterre," *Bibliothèque d'Humanisme et Renaissance*. 15: pp. 15-44.

Lea, Henry C. 1907. *A History of the Inquisition in Spain.* (v 3-4, London-New York).

129

Lecler, Joseph. 1960. *Toleration and the Reformation.* T. L. Westow, transl. (2 v, New York).

Lehnemann, Johannes. 1725. *Historische Nachricht von det Evangelisch Lutherischen Kirche in Antorff* (Frankfurt).

Linnhoff, Liselotte. 1934. *Spanische Protestanten und England* (Emsdetten).

Longhurst, John E. 1960. " Julían Hernández, Protestant Martyr," *Bibliothèque d'Humanisme et Renaissance* 22: pp. 90-118.

Malvezin, Théophile. 1875. *Histoire des juifs à Bordeaux* (Bordeaux).

— 1892. *Histoire du Commerce de Bordeaux depuis les origines jusqu'à nos jours* (v 2, Bordeaux).

Pinette, G. L. 1957. " Die Spanier und Spanien im Urteil des deutschen Volkes zur Zeit der Reformation," *Archiv für Reformationsgeschite* 48: pp. 182-191.

Porter, H. C. 1958. *Reformation and Reaction in Tudor Cambridge* (Cambridge, Eng.).

Purnell, E. K. 1904. *University of Cambridge, College Histories: Magdalene College* (London).

Rahlenbeck, Charles. 1887. "Jean Taffin," *BCHEW* 2: pp. 117-179.

— 1857. *L'Iquisition et la Réforme en Belgique* (Brussels).

Rosenberg, Eleanor. 1955. *Leicester, Patron of Letters* (New York).

Schäfer, Ernest. 1902. *Geschichte des Spanischen Protestantismus und die Inquisition* (3 v, Gütersloh)

Schickler, F. de. 1892. *Les Églises du refuge en Angleterre* (3 v, Paris).

Sepp, Christian. 1875. *Geschkiedkundige Nasporigen* (3 v, Leiden).

— 1885. *Kerkhistorische Studiën* (Leiden).

— 1881. *Polemische on Irenische Theologie* (Leiden).

— 1890 *Uit het Predikantleven van vroegere Tijden* (Leiden).

Stoughton, John. 1883. *The Spanish Reformers* (London).

Strype, John, 1824. *Annals of the Reformation* (4 v in 7, Oxford).

— 1701. *Historical Collections of the Life and Acts of John Aylmer* (London).

— 1710. *History of the Life and Acts of Edmund Grindal* (London).

— 1821. *Life and Acts of Matthew Parker* (3 v, Oxford).

Tollin, Henri N. 1882-1883. " Cassiodoro de Reina," *BSHPF* 31: pp. 385-397; 32: pp. 241-250.

Ungerer, Gustav. 1956. *Anglo-Spanish Relations in Tuder Literature.* (Bern-Madrid).

— 1965. " The Printing of Spanish Books in Elizabethan England," *The Library* Ser. 5 20: pp. 177-229.

Van Lennep, M. 1901. *De Hervorming in Spanje* (Haarlem).

Venn, J. and J. A. 1927. *Alumni Cantabrigiensis* (Cambridge, Eng.).

Venn, John. 1910. *Grace Book.* (Cambridge, Eng.).

Van Schelven, A. A. 1911. " Cassiodorus de Reyna, Christophorus Fabricius on Gaspar Olevianus," *Nederlandsch Archief voor Kerkgeschiedenis* 8: pp. 322-332.

Vuilleumier, Henri. 1927. *Histoire de l'Église réformée du Pays de Vaud sous le régime bernois* (v 1, Lausanne).

Wood, Anthony à. 1794. *History and Antiquities of the University of Oxford* (v 2 i, Oxford).

Hurstfield, Joel. 1962. " Some Elizabethans," *History* 47: pp. 18-31.

Jones, W. M. 1958-1959. " Foreign Teachers in Sixteenth Century England," *The Historian* 21: pp. 162-175.

UNPUBLISHED SOURCES

McFadden, William. 1953. " Life and Works of Antonio del Corro," (Unpublished PhD. thesis, Belfast).

INDEX

137

FOOTNOTE ADDITIONS

14, p. 29   This famous quarrel is more recently summarized by Robert M. Kingdon, *Geneva and the Coming of the Wars of Religion to France, 1555-1563* (Geneva, 1956): p. 21f. Pt. I provides a thorough description of the training, discipline, and placement of missionaries; pp. 38ff show how they slipped into France; pp. 101ff analyze book-smuggling.

57, p. 31   Walzer: pp. 68ff, 307ff, has a judicious analysis of why Calvinism appealed to certain aristocrats, such as Renée; basically he believes it was a leader-oriented religion which would be attractive to those of the upper classes discontented with themselves or their society or both. Kingdon implies as much in his analysis of the Company of Pastors: ch.1. The point always to bear in mind, as these authors see, is that this approach cannot be conclusive, much less all-embracing. Walzer's remark cited in the Preface, n4, sums it up well.

5. p. 71   This is a particularly fascinating viewpoint, which Cousin and his allies never abandoned anymore than Corro surrended his ' open ' outlook on ' outside ' readings. Interestingly, according to Kingdon: p. 16, who came to this observation after studying the private collections of Calvinists, " Calvin's disciples [at least] during his lifetime, were free to read widely among the works of the other great thinkers of the century [he cites Luther as an example] ... Chambeli's ... books [for instance] demonstrate how much *radical* theology students absorbed at Geneva and Lausanne ". My italics.

71, p. 75   It is interesting to note that just after receiving Corro's letter Huntingdon became President of the Council of the North where with Grindal, now at the see of York, he undertook a vigorous campaign against recusancy. This should be recalled when we encounter charges of " crypto-Catholicism " against Corro; it was most unlikely that such enemies of the old faith would have so readily supported him if this had ever had any substance. For Huntingdon and Grindal in the north in this context see Trimble: p. 66. Like Leicester Huntingdon was also a kind of political Puritan I have described below; cf. Walzer: p. 122.

79. p. 76   Trimble: pp. 58ff importantly notes that Cecil ordered an inquiry into this problem in 1569, and p. 86f shows its recurrence in the late ' 70 ' s.

91, p. 76   See Trimble: p. 91 for Catholics at Oxford and Cambridge at this time.

95, p. 76   Walzer: ch. 4 has a fine analysis of what the Puritan doctors were driving for, and on p. 140f, summing up recent research by Curtis, et al, on the universities, he suggests that in this period the Anglican (Proto-Arminian?)—Puritan battle was in fact over control of the education of the country's future leaders.

*Achevé d'imprimé
sur les presses de
l'Imprimerie du « Journal de Genève »
en août 1967
pour le compte des Editions Droz S.A.*

27 101